Advice From The Top

Advice From The Top

The Business Strategies of Britain's Corporate Leaders

Derek Ezra & David Oates

David & Charles
Newton Abbot London

British Library Cataloguing in Publication Data

Ezra, *Sir*, Derek, *1919–*
Advice from the top.
1. Great Britain. Business firms. Management
I. Title II. Oates, David
658′.00941

ISBN 0-7153-9149-6

Printed in Great Britain
by Billings and Sons Worcester
for David & Charles Publishers plc
Brunel House Newton Abbot Devon

Contents

Introduction

by

Derek Ezra

We are living through one of the most exciting periods of change in British industry. In retrospect its impact may well be compared with that of the industrial revolution of the eighteenth and nineteenth centuries. This change has been brought about by a number of factors, some external, some internal. The oil price increases, especially those of 1979, the subsequent recession of 1980 and 1981, the escalation of inflation and unemployment, the impact of new technologies, the application of remedial policies leading to renewed growth – all these have contributed to the rapid economic changes now occurring.

But one factor of special importance has been the contribution and the stimulus of those who have come to the fore in industry during the period. In this book twelve distinguished business leaders talk frankly to David Oates, a much experienced writer and observer of the business scene, about how they rose to the top of their chosen fields and about the strategies that kept them there, in some cases for thirty years or more. They give their views about such crucial issues as leadership, delegation, strategic planning, teamwork, the management of people, social responsibility and how to deal with crises. They come from a wide variety of backgrounds and have performed an extensive range of duties. They illustrate the great diversity and scope of business operations.

Until his recent retirement, Austin Pearce, for example, had spent most of his more than thirty years as a professional manager in the top echelons of industry. He ran Esso for many years and was involved in both the nationalisation and the privatisation of British Aerospace, latterly as its chairman.

Francis Tombs and Robert Haslam have also had exceptional experience in running large enterprises in both the public and the private sectors. Indeed it can be said that in Britain today there is a breed of top managers who have effectively bridged the gap between public and private enterprise, and have succeeded in both sectors. Monty Finniston, having made his mark in the steel industry, has since engaged in a large number of different activities with remarkable and sustained dynamism.

By contrast, Peter de Savary's more instinctive entrepreneurial style has served him well in establishing companies of importance in the oil and leisure sectors. His is an opportunistic approach which takes advantage of the peaks and troughs in more established industries. He was said to have purchased Land's End for just under £7m on little more than a whim when he saw the chance to develop the rugged Cornish landmark into an attractive tourist spot. He has turned Falmouth into the base for an even more exciting venture – his challenge for the coveted America's Cup, the yachting world's most prestigious prize.

De Savary stresses the need to weigh up the risk-reward ratio before embarking on a new venture and most, if not all, the featured business leaders have undertaken perilous risks in the course of their careers. Austin Pearce once defied serious injury, and possibly even death, when he climbed a chimney stack at Esso's Southampton refinery to light a flare which refused to ignite by any other more prudent method. Anita Roddick founded her Body Shop on a £4,000 loan. By all the rules of commerce, such under-capitalisation should have led to failure. But hard work and an irrepressible will to succeed ensured that she built up a business empire that now has a presence in thirty countries. The Body Shop has recently been cited in two major surveys as one of the fastest growing up-and-coming businesses in the world.

Dogged determination also played a crucial role in John Cuckney's fight to save the ailing Westland Helicopter company. He admits that he nearly wore out his worry beads when the rescue plan he mounted as chairman of Britain's only helicopter manufacturer caused a government rumpus and led to the resignation of two cabinet ministers. But by sticking steadfastly to business principles and following the path that best benefitted the shareholders and the employees, he ensured that Westland lived to see another day.

Terence Conran, too, has had his fair share of setbacks in recent years. He has had to hold tight to the reins of leadership as his Storehouse group was besieged by two unwelcome take-over bidders. He had to face the prospect of seeing the years of effort invested in building up a homogeneous retail empire, based on his unique flair for design, come under threat from City institutions which seemed to him to be motivated merely by financial opportunism.

There could hardly be any greater disaster for a fledgling airline than to lose its only aircraft in an accident that claimed the lives of everyone on board. That was the inauspicious birth experienced by British Caledonian, which was nevertheless built up into the major 'second-force' airline in Britain until it finally succumbed to the inevitable and became absorbed into British Airways. There are few more dogged than the Scots, and Adam Thomson battled long and hard to safeguard the independence of his airline until being forced to recognise that trends in the aviation business were steeped too heavily against him.

It could be argued that those captains of industry who were born into established family firms were highly privileged and enjoyed a distinct advantage over those who had to make their own way in the industrial world. But as Hector Laing points out in this book, it is a great responsibility to take charge of an enterprise that has already been turned into a success story by your forebears. It would be hard to deny that he took his responsibilities very seriously. When he joined the family business of McVitie & Price in 1947, it was capitalised at £4m. United Biscuits, as it has now become, is today capitalised at around £1.4bn. The company produces five billion food packages every year – one for every person on earth. Each week it churns out biscuits equivalent in weight to 1,200 elephants. If the group's total annual output in biscuits were placed end to end, it would stretch twice to the moon and back, or forty-eight times around the equator. Sir Hector has certainly not let his inheritance stand idle.

Similarly, Adrian Cadbury has been instrumental in seeing the family chocolate firm grow into a worldwide confectionery and soft drinks concern that is now being eyed enviously by acquisitive predators.

The achievements of the twelve industry leaders outlined in this book are all the more remarkable when set against the turbulent times in which their companies have been passing through. Most captains of industry have been subjected to, and to some degree, suffered from, the impact of 'Big Bang' and the fundamental changes that have taken place in the money markets. As John Cuckney observes:

> I think we in Europe have been a bit slow to recognise that we are in a totally new era. With all the new techniques now available, such as twenty-four hour trading and the global marketing of securities, we have been a bit slow to adapt to changes that are now going to be permanent.

Several of the industrial leaders featured here feel that the pressures resulting from the exponential expansion of financial services are leading to a deterioration in business ethics. Hector Laing, for example, has drawn up a code of ethics for his managers which stresses that 'no one has to take short cuts ever'. He believes the switch from private to institutional shareholding is at the root of many of the problems. 'Fund managers are intent on doing their best for the funds and have no interest whatsoever in the businesses they invest in or the people who produce the profits,' he declares.

Adrian Cadbury, too, is aware of the fast-changing environment in which industrial leaders now have to operate.

> I think the pressures have changed enormously since I started work. The big change is that literally the market place is now global. This seems to me to be an enormous change . . . You get an abrupt rise in the size of firms. It's very difficult then to exercise the same kind of partnership control which traditionally those firms had. So you get a breakdown in the structure.

Austin Pearce advocates a calm response to such pressures and a recognition of human limitations.

> You've got to deal with different problems, there's no question about that. They're on a worldwide scale rather than a national scale, but you have to recognise that there are only so many hours in the day in which you can be efficient.

Keeping a cool head in a turbulent world is the mark of a true corporate leader, but many other qualities are required, as this book aptly illustrates. A top leader needs to have a clear strategy of where he wants his organisation to go and the ability to communicate that strategy to his fellow managers and his work-force. He needs to know when to delegate and to be able to judge those who are capable of taking on devolved responsibility. He needs to be 'visible' in the way he goes about involving his troops. He must demonstrate his interest in what his employees are trying to achieve by moving among them, rather than dictating aloof memos from remote skyscraper offices. He must have the willpower to stick to decisions once they are made, however painful they may be in execution. He should nevertheless be conscious at all times that people are the life force behind businesses and that accommodating their needs as far as is humanly possible will make the difference between success and failure. In addition, he must have the vision to view his company's aspirations in global terms and relate them to the prevailing trends in world markets. That also means being clear about the role his organisation plays in society as a whole and the contribution it should make to public causes.

These are all issues with which our chosen captains of industry have had to grapple during the course of their careers at the helm of some of this country's largest companies and some of its newest companies. The extent to which they have succeeded in taking account of the many demands placed on an industrial leader can perhaps be measured by the fact that they have been in the forefront of a rejuvenation of British industry which is making an increasingly noticed impact on the rest of the world.

This book comprises the frankly stated experiences and motivations of those who have been involved in guiding large enterprises, whether in the public or private sectors, those who have massively expanded family firms, those who have launched into entirely new enterprises and those who have brought ailing businesses back to health. This is the stuff and variety of business enterprise. It could be held, as Monty Finniston does, that it is not so much the nature of the business as the people in it that matters. 'People,' he says, 'are the only appreciating assets you have in business. All the other assets disappear; you write them off . . . In five years a machine is counted as nothing in the balance sheet, but people count and age makes them more experienced, gives them better judgement.' This book is about people who have put their unmistakable stamp on the businesses they have led.

As someone who has been involved for many years in the management of a large public enterprise and subsequently in a diversity of private-sector undertakings, I have been fascinated by what has emerged from these interviews. Many of the problems mentioned are similar to those I have encountered. Naturally I have been specially interested in those who have been involved in large businesses, because that is where I have had my main experience. So I have read with particular care the interviews with Monty Finniston, Robert Haslam, Austin Pearce, Francis Tombs and Graham Wilkins. I have been struck by one thing above all – their air of calmness and detachment when dealing with the many difficulties large businesses inevitably bring in their train. Robert Haslam puts this well when facing a sudden collapse in the market as head of the Fibres Division of ICI: 'The most important thing was just physically keeping up the morale. I had almost consciously to go out of the house in the morning with a fixed smile on my face . . . and breathe an air of absolute confidence.' Graham Wilkins speaks similarly when he took over the chairmanship of the troubled Thorn-EMI: 'The first task, of course, was to put some morale back into the business, because they were in dead trouble.'

But I have found much also in other interviews that has opened up new perspectives – the almost uncanny grasp of opportunities by entrepreneurs such as Peter de Savary; the commitment, through thick and thin, to an ideal, such as shown by Anita Roddick, Adam Thomson and Terence Conran; the exceptional skills of those who have nursed ailing companies back to health, such as Francis Tombs, John Cuckney and Graham Wilkins; the remarkable dedication to family businesses shown by Adrian Cadbury and Hector Laing.

This is more than just a record of achievements by a

selection of successful business leaders. It is a testimony to the enormous changes taking place in British industry today and to those who helped to shape those changes. And it is a challenge to others, reading and pondering over the interviews, to make use of these valuable experiences in building up their own achievements.

Sir Adrian Cadbury

Born: Birmingham, 1929.
Educated: Eton; King's College, Cambridge.

Sir Adrian Cadbury is chairman of Cadbury Schweppes plc. He joined Cadbury Brothers Ltd in 1952 and became chairman in 1965. After the merger between Cadbury and Schweppes he succeeded Lord Watkinson as chairman of the combined company at the end of 1974. He was knighted for his services to industry in 1977.

He is a director of the Bank of England and of IBM UK Holdings Ltd, and chairman of Pro Ned, an organisation that encourages the appointment of non-executive directors to company boards. He also heads the CBI Business Education Task Force.

He is chancellor of the University of Aston in Birmingham, a trustee of the Bournville Village Trust and president of the Birmingham Chamber of Industry and Commerce. He was made a freeman of the City of Birmingham in 1982.

Sir Adrian Cadbury is not one of those who subscribes to the popular theory that a truly professional manager can take over the helm of any type of business with only a superficial knowledge of the nuts and bolts.

> I'm very sceptical of the ability to shift from managing a bank to managing a steel mill, for example. I have grave doubts about that. I think it is essential to understand the key factors for success or failure in your type of business and I'm not convinced you can do that without actually understanding the process in some detail.

For that reason, Sir Adrian looks back with gratitude on the job-rotation policy that was an integral part of basic training when he joined the family firm after coming down from Cambridge in 1952. He found the experience of working in a wide variety of company departments invaluable and believes it held him in good stead when he reached the higher echelons of management. There was a strict system of career development at Cadbury's in those days. About six other Cambridge graduates joined the firm with Sir Adrian and they were put under the protective wing of the head of the employment department, who guided their career progression. It was a firm edict of company policy that all new recruits with management potential should undergo the experience of working temporarily in as many company departments as possible.

> I spent the first eighteen months working in all the factory departments, so I started with a good knowledge of precisely how the product was made and did all the jobs that then existed in the production of confectionery. Everyone did some time in the factory. I did longer than most and it had the advantage that, given there was much greater stability of employment then, I got to know a very large number of people.

He next moved on to the buying office, a very important department in a company such as Cadbury's where the skilful purchase of the ingredients that go into the products can have a crucial impact on the viability of the business. Sir Adrian found this work fascinating and would have been perfectly happy at the time to have made it his long-standing job. But the company's rotation policy dictated that he should be moved 'rather abruptly' into the wages department, where he played a role in setting and negotiating piece rates.

> We had a large factory at Bournville employing about ten thousand people and there were a great many incentive payment schemes, so that became my job. I hadn't asked to do it, but in fact found it very interesting and that took me as a result into trade union negotiations and finally into becoming personnel director.

As he progressed in the company, Sir Adrian also spent time out in the field selling.

> All of us who were not on the sales and marketing side spent a day a month selling. We were given a sales territory. So for the rest of the month I was in charge of wages, piece rates, training, negotiations and all the rest of it, and then one day a month I was regularly calling on the same customers in Bloomsbury and I was collecting money, selling the goods and so on, which I think was a very important part of my continued training.

This varied experience served to convince Sir Adrian that no top executive can really be successful without an in-depth understanding of the finer points of a company's operations.

> I worry about what was certainly a facet of the past in this country – a view that you could be a professional director of dozens of companies. All of that to me smacks of a lack of appreciation of the need to understand a business thoroughly, where you're going to be involved in making major decisions. I also think it's a question of being able to provide, certainly at the top of a company, a sense of direction and I find it hard to see how you can have an absolutely clear sense of direction unless you yourself are able to assess the essentials as you see them for success in your particular trade.

The basic grounding that all new management recruits underwent on joining Cadbury's helped to ensure that each of them obtained this innate understanding. Members of the Cadbury family did not escape this strict initial training. There was no automatic ticket to senior management.

> We were a big family, so there were never any guarantees that members of the family would progress. The arrangement was that they were happy for members of the family to come into the business and, in a sense, find their own level. What is perhaps unusual for a family business was that we had members of the family at very different levels

> in the company. One of my cousins was a senior foreman by the grading of the day. Another was a sales manager. The one who was the senior foreman never moved beyond that grade.

In fact, Sir Adrian had no preconceived ideas about the sort of career he would follow when he came down from Cambridge with a degree in economics. It was perhaps a foregone conclusion that he would go into the family firm founded by his great-grandfather, John Cadbury, in 1824, although he had two tempting offers from outside industry when he had completed his degree. One offer he describes as 'managing quite a lot of money' and the other was a partnership in a substantial firm of solicitors. He rejected them both in favour of joining the family firm, but he was vague about the specific role he would play.

> It was a conscious choice that I wanted to go into the company, but I didn't have a clear view as to what particular part of the business I was interested in. It just seemed like an interesting challenge. At that time it was very much more of a family firm than it is now. It was then called Cadbury Brothers. The title of the holding company was The British Cocoa and Chocolate Company and my father was the chairman. There were a number of other members of the family on the board.

The economic climate in Britain was very different then to what it is today. Sir Adrian believes that today young people aspiring to careers in industry should seriously think about setting up their own small firms. But there was no such enterprise culture in Britain in those days.

> Very few of my contemporaries thought of starting up on their own. So it seemed a fairly straightforward move to go and work for the family firm. It was an entirely different climate from today. Food was still rationed and it was very much a question of making the best use of available resources and we had absolutely unlimited demand – a very false situation as it turned out when you think about what happened to British industry afterwards.

One of the qualities Sir Adrian came to regard as essential as he gained experience of the family firm and aspired to become chairman of Cadbury Schweppes plc was integrity. 'I don't see how you can expect people to follow your lead, to trust you, to commit themselves to the business unless they believe that all of these things are dear to your heart.' He is more hesitant, however, about including an aptitude for leadership among the prerequisites for a successful captain of industry.

> I'm always a little cautious about leadership, because I'm never absolutely certain what it means. There is a connotation to leadership that needs perhaps getting out of the way. The real question, it seems to me, is the sense of direction a leader has. It doesn't seem the slightest use having leadership if you're leading in the wrong direction.

Sir Adrian cites the example of the army commander who leads his troops over the top of of the trenches when it might have been more prudent to stay put. Reckless heroism, very clearly, is not the sort of quality he admires. He doesn't entirely dismiss leadership as a meaningless term, however. 'I totally accept that what you need is the ability to get people to believe in the vision that you put forward of the company, to accept it and to be willing to work towards it. That does seem to me to be important.'

Sir Adrian seems unhappy with the idea of drawing up a vast catalogue of top management attributes and is more inclined to the view that being a good senior executive is something gleaned from hard experience. Although he is a thoughtful person, who loves to put his ideas down on paper in the form of articles for such august publications as the *Harvard Business Review*, he suspects that labels are attached to management practices in hindsight rather than as objectives executives set out to master.

He is sceptical about the plethora of management books that deal in 'grand abstractions'. He is not convinced that having read them aspiring managers can go away and teach themselves to be good leaders. He believes, rather, that such abilities are acquired through a steady upward progression within a company.

> There has to be a period of simply understanding how

things work; then graduating to some degree of management control. I'm not sure you can jump from there to the strategy of the business. I don't think you can miss out any of the intervening stages of progression.

Given that Sir Adrian places so much store by integrity in top management, he views the apparent decline in business morals with some concern.

I believe in the end that one of the casualties of taking short cuts and losing integrity is that you will not get good people coming into the business. At the end of the day, that is what it all turns on. If companies such as our own can be successful while maintaining standards I think we will attract people who will get something worthwhile out of a business career.

Sir Adrian attributes the moral decline largely to pressure brought about by a faster-pace world, particularly in the City where salary levels have become inflated beyond all recognition and where greed can easily take precedence over ethical practice.

I think the pressures have changed enormously since I started work. The big change is that literally the market place is now global. This seems to me to be an enormous change. Curiously, it was actually very slow to happen in the financial services markets. They protected themselves for a long time. Now suddenly it's happened, so you get a lot of new people coming in. You get an abrupt rise in the size of firms. It's very difficult then to exercise the same kind of partnership control which traditionally those firms had. So you get a breakdown in the structure. That is a direct result of the sudden increase in competition and the consequent expansion of the range of services and the size of firms in order to respond to it.

You see the same thing in our kind of business, but we've really been operating in international markets for much longer and it's a slower process. You can see it in our trade obviously in the way in which companies have

> amalgamated and merged and grown. The size of the players has changed. We have to try to make ourselves more efficient and to accept change, but there are certain things we should hang on to.

Rapid changes in the market place put a great strain on top management to ensure a company is keeping pace and is sufficiently aware of what is happening around the world. Sir Adrian believes it is very much the responsibility of a captain of industry to take the lead in such matters and to define the sort of company you want to become. 'It's very difficult to do because if you aren't careful you just write down a series of platitudes, but I think that a statement of aims and beliefs is very necessary even if it does look platitudinous.'

Since the war, Cadbury Schweppes has undergone two fundamental rethinks about the strategy it should adopt. One was in 1969 when the original firm of Cadbury merged with Schweppes, a merger that changed the whole character of the company. A more recent reappraisal took place in the early 1980s when the decision was taken to shed the foods side of the business and concentrate on the confectionery and soft drinks divisions.

> Operating in an international market, what you do is dictated by the moves your competitors in the confectionery and soft drinks markets are making. Against that background, we decided to switch direction. We had previously gone for a somewhat broader base to the business for perfectly good reasons. Developing the food side of the business was a way of making better use of the Cadbury brand. We had an asset in the Cadbury brand, so we spread it across biscuits, cakes and a range of other products. We were getting more mileage out of an asset we already owned and it gave the business a wider base to cope with fluctuations in any part of it.
>
> But it became clear that was not the way to hold our own against companies like Coca-Cola and Pepsi-Cola, or Mars on the confectionery side. Our resources were too widely deployed, which gave us stability, but lost us a competitive edge. So there came a point when it made sense to change that particular balance.

Such major changes of strategy aren't made without sacrifices, and the consequent upheavals took a certain toll at Cadbury's, not least of which was the need to reduce the work-force. This is an issue that is close to Sir Adrian's heart. Having devoted much of his career to the personnel function and having been an ardent advocate of participative management, he talks about such problems with an obvious depth of feeling. He has no hesitation in saying that the most difficult aspects of management for him are those that involve making decisions about people, whether it be a question of promotion, demotion or making somebody redundant. 'Of all business decisions, these are the most worrying,' he maintains. 'You can't be certain you're right and there is the greatest temptation to put them off and not to take them. And obviously you worry about the consequences for the individuals concerned.'

Sir Adrian does feel, however, that companies can take measures to reduce the hardships that redundancy inevitably brings.

> There are ways in which you can soften it. We did in fact get through a very major reduction at Bournville without any forced redundancies. We did it simply by foreseeing the situation and starting the rundown early enough by stopping recruitment. What you need to do is to involve people so they know what has to be done and plan it as far ahead as possible to minimise the impact. But having said that, you have to close sites and obviously that does lead to hardship.

What Sir Adrian is absolutely certain about is that top managers need to be decisive and should not push issues under the rug in the hope they will solve themselves. One of the most difficult decisions he was faced with in recent years was whether or not to sell the foods business, particularly as it involved disposing of Cadbury's Cocoa, the product with which his great-grandfather launched the company. It was a traumatic moment for the chairman. It also epitomises the complexity of business decisions that top managers have to take and the many issues that have to be weighed in the balance before reaching a conclusion. And after that, the implementation of the decision can be equally difficult.

> The first decision was clearly whether it made sense to concentrate all our resources behind the two core businesses, without foods. We kicked that around and in the end, I'm absolutely certain rightly, decided it was better to concentrate our resources. There was then the decision about what should happen to the foods division. We had the possibility both of a management buy-out and of interest from outside the company.

This presented Sir Adrian and his top management team with a dilemma. There is a widely held view among many business experts that selling off a business to a management buy-out team is the easy way out and is not in the best interests of a company's shareholders.

> We had to weigh up the bid which the managers put forward against outside bids and they're never in exactly the same terms. So, in a sense, you're comparing apples with pears. We agonised over the decision before selling to the management and I'm absolutely convinced with hindsight that the decision was not only right in people terms but it was also the right business decision for the shareholders as well.

Part of the deal with the management buy-out team was an option on ten per cent of the new company when it came to the market, no equivalent of which was possible under the terms of any of the outside bids. The buy-out company – Premier Brands – has since been doing well and Sir Adrian is confident Cadbury's shareholders will have nothing to complain about when the new company does eventually go to the market. The decision top management took has been vindicated, but there was some criticism, particularly from City analysts, at the time it was taken. Stressing the complexity of such business decisions, Sir Adrian points out: 'It isn't a question of just saying it's A or B. There are any number of stations between A and B you have to examine.'

Sir Adrian doesn't profess to have any special technique for making up his mind over difficult decisions as some top executives do. He returns to his familiar theme of the need to study issues in depth and to do all the necessary homework. 'All you can do is study the situation as thoroughly as you can and be clear as to what the issues are and who is going to be affected by the decision. The essential thing is that you should do the homework as thoroughly as you can.'

He does, however, condemn procrastination.

> Having done that you have to make up your mind and the great sin, it seems to me, is to put decisions off. One of the things I worry about considerably is that I feel a lot of well-meaning people bring pressure to bear on companies *not* to take decisions. If you go back to the time United Biscuits felt they had to close their Liverpool factory, the bishops up in Liverpool marched on Hector Laing and tried to persuade him to put the decision off. They meant well, but the easiest thing in the world to do is to put difficult decisions off. That really is the primrose path. I don't think the people who advocate these policies understand that you have every wish to put the decision off. Nothing would be pleasanter than not having to make people redundant, not having to close a factory, but your job is to take the decisions when you have assessed the evidence as carefully as you can and not to shirk them.

Sir Adrian is a staunch believer in decisions based on logical analysis, rather than the gut feeling some entrepreneurs prefer to act upon.

> I would find it very hard to follow gut feel if I could not put forward arguments on two sides of a sheet of paper as to why it was the right decision. I like to think things through. I like, before coming to a decision, to get the arguments down on paper and it seems to me if you can't then convince yourself or anybody else that what you propose is logically right, it doesn't much matter what your gut's doing.

Bournville, the community that has grown up around Cadbury's Birmingham factory, is widely regarded as a company town, although from its foundation it has been open to people who do not work for the company and only a minority of the residents now have any link with Cadbury's. But having spent all his career in a family business, Sir Adrian has inevitably given a lot of thought to the responsibility a company should have for the community in which it operates. He nevertheless finds it difficult to define, because there is such a thin dividing line between paternalism and being a good corporate citizen.

> It seems to me you have to start from the fact that your role in the community is to produce goods and services which people want. That's your prime task, which in the end you have to come back to. If you don't do that efficiently then you are not doing a good job for the community. Then you have the problem of reconciling that with other duties, such as your legal duties which tend to lag behind best practice.

He believes that each company needs to set its own targets for being a good corporate citizen, which can range from how much money should be donated to charities to making senior executives available for secondment to advise small businesses.

> In one sense, businesses are licensed by the community to operate and you have to work within the terms of the licence, which tend to change. You have to keep in tune with the changes. After all, it wasn't that long ago that it was quite acceptable to belch smoke over the countryside. The responsibility can be defined differently at different periods of time.
>
> It's very easy within our own company to see the stages that Cadbury has gone through. My grandfather built the village in 1895 – not as a company town. It was open to everybody, but clearly it was convenient for people working in the place. He built it for a very simple reason. Not because he wanted to set up a model village, but because he saw that with the employment he was generating at Bournville out in the Worcestershire countryside, speculative builders would come in and put up very inferior dwellings if he didn't take a hand. So he bought the land around the factory, and the village now covers one thousand acres. But it was with a very clear purpose. It was to prevent bad development and to show that you could build decent houses with gardens at

> rents people could afford and also that you could develop a community, which is why he was never in favour of a company town. He set the village up as a separate body even then under a charitable trust, which it continues to be to this day. Obviously the gap between the two has grown through time.

In those days, Cadbury's saw it as part of its social responsibility to provide training and education for the workers it recruited. When Sir Adrian joined the company it was compulsory for all young people up to the age of eighteen to spend a day a week at the company's continuation college.

> That seemed to me to be a perfectly proper use of what the company had to offer. It meant we got good recruits. Now the world has changed. In the early 1960s it became clear that compulsory continuing education was actually becoming a hindrance to recruitment. Fewer people were coming forward to take jobs because they didn't like having to go to school. So continuing education became voluntary and therefore the dividing line between what is paternalistic or not is constantly shifting.

There is no doubt in Sir Adrian's mind that it is more demanding today being a top executive than it used to be. Running a large company has become far more complex, which is aggravated by the rapid pace of change, in his view. But he believes that there are developments around the corner that could bring a lot of changes for the better, not least of them, technological changes. He believes such innovations as 'distance working', which will enable people to operate from home 'instead of having to converge on places in order to work', will offer all kinds of promise for improving some of the less agreeable aspects of a business career. He fondly hopes that in the meantime talented managers won't be deterred from seeking to take on top jobs because of the greater demands. 'It seems to me that people who worry about their responsibilities and mind about the consequences of their actions should be prepared to take senior jobs. It would be a very sad day if that wasn't the case.'

He believes that talk of the so-called 'post-industrial society' is raising some unnecessary fears that may be causing some talented managers to have second thoughts about aspiring to a top job. Like a lot of top executives in manufacturing industries, he believes the repercussions of a predicted major shift towards the service industries to be grossly exaggerated. 'I'm sceptical about what post-industrial means. It sounds suspiciously like getting everything without working for it. I think the fundamentals will stay the same.'

He does accept, however, that automation will continue to eat away at jobs and leave top executives with agonisingly difficult decisions and that this is bound to make their jobs more stressful. He believes it will call for a fundamental rethink about the way that work is structured.

> I think there will be far more job-sharing. I think people, if they have any sense, will work shorter hours. Some will follow the example of Arthur C. Clarke, who has retired to Sri Lanka, because he says he can work better there, can enjoy the environment and is just as close to his numerous correspondents as if he were in America.

Sir Adrian utterly rejects the definition of work as full-time employment. He fervently believes we must all become accustomed to more flexible lives in which work, education and training are all intermingled.

> Most of us will be working part time and voluntary work will be considered work just as much as paid work and in that way we can distribute the enormous amount of work that needs to be done more evenly. It's absurd really to say that because of automation there is less and less work when you see how much there is that needs doing in the community. I think we will balance work and leisure in a totally different way.

Sir Adrian personally believes there is a lot of satisfaction to be derived from being a top executive, although he spurns the more visible trappings of success. 'I have no interest in fast cars. I don't have a yacht or a second home,' he points out. His pleasure comes from a different source: 'I am obviously very conscious of what my forebears achieved and therefore it matters to me that the business has survived, remained independent and has grown.'

He has tried hard to balance his managerial duties with outside interests and not to allow himself to become too much of a workaholic. But that has led to him becoming involved in an 'appalling number' of outside bodies, in addition to being chancellor of Aston University and a trustee of the Bournville village. 'If I were to go to only one meeting a year for each of them, it would still be more than one a week,' he confesses, admitting that it is one of his greatest weaknesses. He writes most of his articles at home, however. 'I may not be as much with my family as I should be, but at least I am at home,' he reasons.

His love of writing, he believes, stems from his analytical training at university. 'I like thinking something through and then setting it down on paper. It puts my mind at rest. I feel I have worked it out of my system.' There may be similar reasons for his love of gardening. 'I think I've got a tidy mind,' he volunteers.

He used to be a keen sportsman in his younger days and rowed for England. He still takes an active interest in Henley Regatta, where he is a steward. 'I need to do physical work in fact', he says.

Most of the outside organisations he is involved with are based in the Midlands. 'I get satisfaction from being able to be involved in a number of activities in the part of the world where I live and have my roots.'

His three children have all made their own way in the world, preferring not to join the family firm. But what advice would he pass on to any young person with their sights set on a career in industry?

> I would tell them that they should study something in depth and really understand it. I don't think it matters much what you study, but I think to do so is very important in terms of promoting the power to think about issues. I wouldn't be too worried whether people do that at university or not. The idea that we should divide our lives into three parts – education/full-time work/retirement – seems to me to be absurd. The ability to return to education at later stages in one's life is something that is very important and I hope will

be encouraged. Nevertheless, I would advocate studying some subject in depth, not necessarily as an undergraduate, so that you can feel you have really mastered it at some stage in your career.

I believe you should understand the mechanics and the principles of the business you want to take up, whether it's a profession or a service or manufacturing. The only thing I would add is that you need to find out what you are good at; you need to find out what it is you can contribute which other people can't and that is something which only you can find out for yourself.

Sir Terence Conran

Born: London, 1931.
Educated: Bryanston School, Dorset; the Central School of Art and Design, London.

Sir Terence Conran is chairman and chief executive of Storehouse plc, the £1.5bn retailing group formed when British Home Stores merged with Habitat Mothercare in January 1986. The group employs some 33,000 people and has over 950 outlets, excluding franchises.

Conran was one of the designers involved in the Festival of Britain in 1951. He set up as a freelance industrial designer making furniture from a basement studio in 1952. In 1956 the Conran Design Group was added, now one of the largest design organisations in Europe. He began his retailing career in 1964 when he founded Habitat, a chain of stores selling well-designed modern furniture and furnishings.

In October 1981 he floated the company on the Stock Exchange and four months later he merged Habitat with Mothercare, the world's largest chain of stores catering for the needs of mothers and babies, and became chairman of the Habitat Mothercare Group plc. In April 1983 this group acquired Heal & Son, the long-established and well-known furnishers. In September 1983, Habitat Mothercare embarked on a joint publishing venture with Octopus Books plc under the name of Conran Octopus Ltd. A range of books has been launched which reflects his design philosophy and style.

In September 1983 Habitat Mothercare joined with merchant bankers Morgan Grenfell to purchase the Richard Shops chain. Three years later Storehouse acquired Morgan Grenfell's forty-eight per cent stake in Richards. In June 1985 Habitat Mothercare, in conjunction with a major French insurance company, acquired the majority shareholding in the French retailing company, FNAC.

In April 1987, Storehouse plc, in a joint venture with the Pamplemousse Clothing Company, opened seven Anonymous stores in the London area, selling stylish fashions for the eighteen- to thirty-year-old woman. In December 1987, Storehouse balanced its women's fashion business with the purchase of Blazer, the successful menswear chain specialising in classic English style.

In 1983, Conran was presented with The Royal Society of Arts Bicentenary Medal, awarded to designers who have 'exerted an exceptional influence in promoting art and design in British industry'. He received his knighthood in the 1983 Queen's New Year's Honours List.

'Did it ever occur to you that everything in this world has had to be designed?' asks Sir Terence Conran, pausing for the significance of his question to sink in. There is a hint of impatience in the tone of his voice. He is clearly rather tired of preaching the design gospel when it has been evident to him for many years the fundamental role it plays in good business practice.

Ever since Conran converted a struggling furniture-manufacturing business into a unique chain of retail shops called Habitat and set in motion a high-street revolution, good design has been at the core of everything he has done. It has taken the rest of industry in this country a remarkably long time to come around to his viewpoint, but it is finally looking as though the penny has dropped.

> Until fairly recently I don't think people have understood the design process or what it can do for the success of their companies. Design is about the way a product not only looks, but also functions, and for anybody in manufacturing industry or retailing to say they don't take an interest in it would be perfectly ludicrous, because at the end of the day it is design that causes a product either to be successful or unsuccessful.
>
> There is nothing manufactured by man that has not been designed, because whether it's a Rolls-Royce engine or a piece of printed paper, there's always a decision to be made

> not only about what it's going to look like but about how it is going to be made and how it is going to operate. That is what design is. Everybody's been doing it, but they've not thought about it as a design process and they have not usually brought people with design skills into the team to make these things happen better. Everybody obviously can design something. We are designers simply in the way we write our name on a piece of paper. It may be unconscious, but we've made a decision at some stage about how it's going to be. So in my view design is absolutely fundamental and at the very core of most businesses.

Conran, whose own highly successful application of design to a flourishing business speaks for itself, explodes the myth that it is a mystical process, largely to do with aesthetic qualities dreamed up by artistic types with a special vision denied to most of us. In his view, design is ninety-eight per cent commonsense and two per cent a magic ingredient to do with aesthetics. Some would say that Habitat used the two per cent to great effect in creating a unique style of goods that appealed to the popular taste. But Conran claims that it was the application of the commonsense element of design that was primarily responsible for the retail group's eventual runaway success. It was, he maintains, the complete reversal in the manufacturer-retailer relationship where design is concerned that brought about the high-street revolution for which Habitat was largely responsible.

> The great change that has occurred is that retailers no longer go out into the market place and buy what is offered to them by manufacturers. They go now with a much greater knowledge of their customers to manufacturers and say: 'We want our products to be made like this for us and we want them to be our products.' In other words, they're taking a lot of the task that used to be given to manufacturers away from them and so manufacturers today are not by and large so concerned with manufacturing brands which are their own and will sit on retailers' shelves as with providing a product for a retailer who wants to construct his own brand.

Conran has been steeped in design from his early years. He

trained at the Central School of Art and Design, but never graduated, joining instead a group of frustrated designers, which included such budding innovationists as Mary Quant and Laura Ashley, who, like Conran himself, were eventually to become household names. Conran ran a café selling 4p bowls of soup and a King's Road coffee bar to help raise the capital to start up his own furniture-manufacturing business, which turned out products similar to those found in Habitat shops today. He first ventured into retailing in 1964 because he was so disenchanted with the way his furniture was being displayed in the shops to which he supplied. It was often buried away among Regency reproduction furniture in shops which were empty most of the time. One spring Conran went on a tour of sixty shops which sold his furniture. He was appalled by the lack of imagination and innovation in the way the furniture was displayed.

To show the trade how furniture should be displayed he opened his first Habitat in the Fulham Road in London. But first he analysed what was wrong with the established shops. 'People buy furniture infrequently and therefore go into the shop very rarely. That's why they are nearly always empty,' he explained in an interview with *Your Business* magazine in 1984.

> We asked ourselves what we could do to make the shops busy. The answer was to sell other things in the same style: china, lighting, textiles, rugs and kitchenware. But we had no idea it would become a chain of shops.
>
> It was the moment when there was new interest in cooking in this country, but nowhere to buy kitchen equipment. So we went to France to this huge warehouse in Les Halles. There were stacks of things being sold to the French restaurant trade which were perfect for us. But we were so hopelessly naïve we didn't realise we were buying at retail prices. All we got was a small discount because we bought such a huge quantity.

Despite such naïvety, the concept that was to give Habitat a unique position in Britain's retailing trade was born. Conran had launched a business empire that was eventually to employ thirty-three thousand people. The growth was far from meteoric, however. After an unsuccessful merger with Ryman, the office equipment chain, Conran bought back the Habitat name and shops. The 1970s were the boom years. His empire mushroomed across Britain, France and the USA. It went public in 1981. Months later it merged with the considerably larger Mothercare chain in a reverse take-over. The upmarket London furniture store Heals, fashion chain Richard Shops and finally British Home Stores were absorbed into the group, which eventually became known as the Storehouse group.

It is rare in British industry for a designer to become the head of such a large business, and Conran can sometimes appear defensive about the unusual position in which he finds himself. He argues that if anyone questions the suitability of a designer as a captain of industry it displays the lack of understanding about the true nature of design that has plagued this country for many years. He maintains that the same rational decision-making process that applies to any design project applies equally to running a business. Arriving at a design for a new product, he insists, entails seeking marketing advice, weighing up how the product is going to be made and manufactured, understanding the cost elements and how it is going to be sold and presented to the customer. 'The majority of a designer's work is simply a rational process. Therefore, why shouldn't a rational person be able to head a company, just the same as a figures man, who is also a rational person?'

Conran also disputes the suggestion that it must be difficult for a man so wrapped up in design to divorce himself from detailed involvement in the creative process in order to tackle the numerous other tasks that befall a captain of industry.

> A designer involved in any industrial process is involved with a team of people. He's involved with the buying side of the business, the marketing side, the production side and probably the advertising side. As chairman of this group, I obviously have financial people, accountants, treasury people, lawyers, personnel people, property people and so on who all make part of a team. It's a different sort of team, but it's a team. So I am used to that process of working as a team and to delegating responsibility to the team and then of course monitoring and checking the results of the team.

Conran is convinced, too, that his experience of manufacturing in the early days has stood him in good stead as head of a retailing empire. He first decided to go into manufacturing because when he finished his design training in the early 1950s there were few jobs available simply because in those days industry, by and large, saw no call for designers. Fortunately for Conran, he had attended the sort of public school 'which had taught me a lot of practical skills'. Going into manufacturing for himself, therefore, was something that came fairly easy to him and for most of the 1950s he built up a substantial furniture business.

> I think the manufacturing experience I had was very important, because it enabled me to see things from the manufacturer's point of view, which many retailers haven't done. Retailers have a tendency to be quite selfish people wanting more and more of a product that is selling well, but cancelling an order and telling you to go away and solve your own problems when there's a product that isn't selling well. Being able to see both points of view has helped me in doing what we are trying to do, namely having things made specially for us and creating our own brands.

Conran's transition from manufacturing to retailing was a gradual process. After he pulled out of the Ryman operation, however, he left manufacturing for good.

> I was quite sorry to do so because I liked the manufacturing process very much indeed, but I don't believe you can be both a manufacturer and a retailer. You can only be one or the other because the whole business of supply and demand is so complex. When I became chairman of Hepworths, it had its own clothing plant and it either produced too much or not enough of the right quality at the right price at the right time. There's always an argument between your own manufacturing company and the retailing side. Another problem is that if you're trying to deal with other manufacturers in the way that we do, where we have this extremely close relationship and they are very reliant on our forward forecasts of volume, they feel if you have

> your own manufacturing plant that you would always give preference to it in bad times and the other suppliers would be the people to suffer if sales declined. The relationship when manufacturing and retailing are in the same company never seems to be a healthy one and I think there are many examples of that.

Leaving manufacturing behind enabled Conran to concentrate on retailing and position his company at the vanguard of the high-street revolution.

> I suppose we were the first people in the 1960s to target our market and bring to people things that were well designed at an affordable price. We probably opened a lot of people's eyes. It is extraordinary that it took so long for the importance of this to be realised in Britain. We were a tiny fumbling company for ten years before anybody took any notice of us. Today, I think people would say that a lot of what we did in those early days has been influential in the general brightening up of the high streets in this country.

Having proved the value of a design-led business, Conran saw the logic of applying the same approach to other retail companies that had perhaps got left behind in the high-street revolution. The take-over of Mothercare, despite the fact it was three times the size of Habitat, seemed to make a lot of sense. The mother and baby specialist retail chain had been very successful in identifying a gap in the market and had filled it very efficiently, but it lacked the flair and creative genius that Conran had brought to Habitat and was losing business as a consequence.

> The reason it was suffering a decline was because its product was no longer meeting the aspirations of the young mums in this country, and while other companies were improving their product ranges Mothercare had become stuck in a groove, because the very competent man who ran it really didn't know how to go about improving the product. He had no skills as a designer. He knew how to get a product that was decent and rather unexciting on to the shop floor, but when it became necessary to add more

to that product and to innovate in design terms, he didn't know how to go about it.

We had very little experience in clothing design at that stage, although we had run a small experiment with Habitat called Clothes Line. But we knew how to bring our design skills into Mothercare, because the design process is very much the same for graphics design or engineering design or for fashion design. It's just a question of finding the right people to bring in and form a fashion-design group. This we did and very soon improved the Mothercare product range with sparkling results. It took us three years to do it, but we changed the face of Mothercare and doubled the profits.

Conran was undaunted by the size of the acquisition. Organisationally, Mothercare was solidly run with all its management systems working well. It had simply lost its way in terms of product innovation, the area in which Habitat had demonstrated itself to be supreme. In addition, Conran's company had by now developed some advanced management systems of its own. In the early 1970s, Habitat was the first retailing company to install electronic point of sale systems (EPOS) in its stock control department for the automatic replenishment of stocks.

The idea was just beginning to catch on in America and we knew that it was going to become *the* way that retailing companies were run. So here was a company run by designers, as people might like to criticise us, putting in the most forward-thinking advanced systems for controlling stock, because it was the logical thing to do - the common-sense thing to do. Provided you choose the right companies to work with and employ the right people to do it, you can get the right results.

It doesn't always go so smoothly. In 1987 there was a complete breakdown of a computerised distribution system in Mothercare, which had been installed by a leading group of experts.

We made the mistake of not having enough of our own practical management to check that they were doing the right thing. You should never assume that because they are the world's greatest experts on retail warehousing that the job can be left entirely to them. You've always got to have it checked out. My favourite cartoon is of a businessman standing in Wall Street selling boxes of matches and around his neck is a placard which says: 'I left it all to expert advice.' It's a very salutary lesson. Employ the right experts, but check it all the time.

In the autumn of 1987, Conran ran into a potentially more serious stumbling block to his plans. The Storehouse group suddenly became the target of unwelcome take-over bids, first from Mountleigh, an ambitious property group, and then from Benlox, a £45m group, twenty-three per cent owned by Egyptian financier Ashraf Marwan, and advised by the *enfant terrible* of merchant banking, Peter Earl of Inficorp Earl, part of Tamwood. There were also rumours that newspaper tycoon Robert Maxwell was showing more than a passing interest in Storehouse. Conran found himself beleaguered and somewhat bemused as to why his group should suddenly be the focal point of so many would-be suitors. His theory about the most likely cause of all the furore is an interesting reflection on the recent workings of the City of London.

I think it's a perfect example of rumour feeding on rumour, that once something gets into the market place it causes all sorts of entrepreneurial people out there to think there's an opportunity they ought not to miss. The City is going through a very muddled stage at the moment – post-Big Bang – forgetting some of its traditional commonsense. I don't want to sound dog-in-the-manger about it, but we have performed reasonably well in quite a difficult retail climate, but a view was put around that the individual companies in the Storehouse group were worth more separately than as a group. Popular theory now decrees that small specialist retail companies get a higher stock-market rating than the big conglomerates, so the latest fashion is for Sock Shops, Body Shops, whatever it is, with very high P/Es, while larger organisations get a lower rating because they are a group.

In fact, the centre of Storehouse is very small. It's about

> thirty people, really that of a very small central overhead, certainly when spread around a company with £1.8bn of sales. Also, we have something that is very unique and that is a design group that provides a design service at arm's length to each of the operating companies. They buy from it and the design group has to look after its own destiny and its own profitability. So what't happening is a lot of rumour out there and a lot of people who think that this is a wonderful opportunity to make ten per cent on the deal.

The rumours were further fuelled by a general statement Conran had previously made about the responsibilities of a group chairman when talking to a journalist. He had said that it was the duty of any chairman to refer an offer that came from a reputable source to his board and shareholders. That had been wrongly interpreted to mean that Conran was actively seeking a suitor. The lesson Conran has learned is never to make general statements to the press that can be quoted out of context and always to keep a weather eye on the latest fads in the City. But in fact there appears to be little a company chairman can do other than try to ride out the fashion of the moment. Conran suspects that the current vogue for de-mergers will eventually turn full circle and there will be a return to the times when it was thought that,

> a collection of targeted retail companies supported by a strong central management core actually is a good thing rather than a bad thing. At one time the City had an enormous enthusiasm for mergers. We were quite a good example with Habitat merging with Mothercare and then taking on Richard Shops, Heals and eventually BHS, all done extremely amicably. We are very likely to see the cycle coming back again.

Conran cites the time when Habitat and other leading British-based retail groups were first entering overseas markets and had a struggle to make profits as another example of the fickle behaviour of City investors. It became the common view that any British retailer attempting to expand abroad signalled a deterioration in its fortunes, with the consequent lack of interest from the City. The City very soon changed its tune, however, when the retailers in the fullness of time proved the wisdom of venturing into overseas markets and ultimately returned good profits.

> The lesson is to stick with what you really believe in. Keep on looking at it all the time. Be aware of what is happening all over the world, but for goodness sake don't allow the market – by which I mean the City – to guide the destiny of your company.

Conran acknowledges that in the face of City rumour it is important for a group such as his to communicate to the outside world what its overall strategy is and to spell out the logic of its master plan – something he feels Storehouse might have done to better effect prior to becoming besieged by unwelcome take-over bids.

> The job of communicating is very important indeed and maybe one of our problems is that we have been doing so much within the business that we are not ready to communicate to the outside world that it perhaps doesn't understand sufficiently what our targets are. You have got to keep the analysts and the institutions on your side and let them know what you're proposing. The problem is that if one of the projects you tell them about goes wrong, as inevitably it will, they're inclined to hold it against you.

Conran admits that he derives little satisfaction from having to fight off unwelcome suitors.

> I find it very depressing because it takes me away from the constructive side of the business and into being a sort of financial PR and being defensive. I'm bad at being defensive. I don't enjoy it. It's not a role that I welcome, although I try hard as a responsible chairman of the group to do the job as well as I possibly can. There are moments of amusement in it. I suppose my main concern in all this is that we employ thirty-three thousand people and their

> lives are being considerably upset by this activity and I feel I am fighting for them as much as for the shareholders.

The Storehouse chairman feels far more at home leading the expansion of the group he has built up so assiduously. He believes it still has a long way to go.

> I don't believe there is such a thing as being able to stop a business in its tracks and say that's far enough. I think there has always got to be for any executive – and for any employee for that matter – new challenges, new frontiers to keep them enthused. They can't go on making the same widget day after day. There's got to be development and opportunities.

Conran has never allowed his job to become mere routine and there is no doubt in his mind about the satisfaction he has derived from building up a business empire.

> I suppose the appeal to me has been making things happen and changing things and feeling quite British about it and proud of what in my very small way I have been able to do in this country and being able to export that abroad and make it a success there. So there's a certain amount of nationalist pride. There were also many years of frustration in my youth when the business was very small and I was bubbling with ideas, bubbling with energy and desperate to get things to happen but couldn't in the very dull environment of the 1950s and early 1960s. So I feel a terrific relief and release that in the latter part of my business life I've been really able to make things happen at a considerable speed.

Surprisingly, the turning point that saw a struggling business transformed into a trendsetting group that has become a household name can be traced back to a Dutch merchant banker, who persuaded Conran to widen his horizons. British merchant banks had failed to see the enormous unfulfilled potential in Habitat and tended to regard it as one of those here-today, gone-tomorrow phenomena. However, the Dutchman, with shrewd insight, saw great prospects for Habitat and persuaded Conran that in order to grow big he had to think big. When the opportunity to acquire Mothercare arose, the Dutchman encouraged Conran to seize it with both hands. 'It just needed somebody to say: "Don't be so humble. You are really much better than you think you are." He opened our eyes to a lot of opportunities.'

With widening horizons, it was inevitable that Conran would turn his attention to expansion abroad. When he was looking to expand into Scotland, Britain was on the verge of joining the Common Market, a move Conran, a staunch European at the time, embraced with great enthusiasm. 'The problems of distribution and the various changes that we had to make to establish ourselves in Scotland made me think that if I just swung the compass I'd land up in Paris.' By coincidence, a manager who spoke good French and understood the French market place had just been recruited. Conran asked this manager to carry out a feasibility study, the result of which convinced him that Habitat should move into France, a country for which he has always had a great fondness.

The group's expansion into the US market was not quite so smooth. The City took a dim view of what it regarded as the inordinate amount of time it took for the group to return a profit there. But Conran had decided not to soft-pedal in the US and had made up his mind to make a big splash immediately, which required large investments which it took years to recoup.

> You can adopt two lines of approach when you start a new business. You can either be very timid and start in a small way, building it up gradually and expecting to make a profit in the first year. Or you can say: I've researched it, I know the idea is right, I'm going to go in big and I'm going to have to sustain four or five years of losses before I turn it into a profit. The trouble about starting a very small business is that it's difficult to do things of any great originality, because you don't have the buying power or maybe the manufacturing base to really get the thing off the ground. That's what I did when I started my furniture business, building it up gradually from a crude workshop and it took a hell of a long time. I didn't get anywhere very fast, but when you are confident and you know the

> market is there it is inevitable, because of the heavy initial investment, that you're going to make substantial losses in the early years. That's the view we've always taken in expanding abroad. We're prepared to sustain losses for several years while we get it going.

While tastes differ from country to country, good design is universal, in Conran's view. The functional qualities of a product are very much the same everywhere and transcend most boundaries. To insure against peculiarities of taste, the Storehouse group has always put its overseas ventures under the control of local managers who tailor the businesses to suit national idiosyncracies. Mistakes are not always avoided, however. When Habitat decided to launch its incredibly successful range of glass tableware in the US, it expected to take the American market by storm. It had overlooked the fact, however, that the Americans tend to be more generous when pouring drinks and like to add large ice cubes to their favourite tipple. The British-made glasses were simply too small to accommodate American tastes.

Conversely, Habitat flew in the face of expert opinion when it introduced pack-flat furniture on to the American market. The pack-flat furniture had been invented recognising that younger people had become more mobile and often did not have the time to wait around at home for furniture deliveries. The pack-flat furniture was easy to transport and could be assembled at home. Habitat was advised that the Americans would never take to this peculiar British invention. But after Habitat set about educating them to the advantages of the idea, the Americans adopted it with tremendous enthusiasm. Habitat is an old hand at changing habits of a lifetime. It was the first company to introduce duvets in both the UK and the US. Few would have dared to predict in the late 1960s that duvets would ever catch on in this country, but today it would be hard to find a British household that doesn't have one.

The Habitat-Mothercare group reduced the risk of offending against local custom when it entered the Japanese market by operating a franchise through an established Japanese retail group called Siebu. The main problem was that all the furniture had to be scaled down to suit the smaller stature of the Japanese and to fit their smaller homes.

Perhaps surprisingly, Conran's management style and operating methods have changed little in the light of his vast experience.

> I suppose the most recent lesson is that if you merge with a company you don't have the same opportunities for changing its culture as you do if it's a take-over. If it's a take-over, you are the boss from day one. If it's a merger there's a gradual shifting of the sands until it finds its own level. I think perhaps in the Habitat-Mothercare-BHS merger things have taken rather longer to settle down than they might have done if it had been a take-over. There are also a lot of advantages in acquisition accountancy which can provide a sort of beer mat for the first years while you are trying to put the businesses together, and of course we didn't have these in the merger. We had merger accountancy rather than take-over accountancy.

Absorbing a merged company into the group presents Conran with one of his most difficult management tasks.

> The most difficult aspect of a merger is trying to put a team together of people who come from different business cultures and trying to adjust them to a different end. It is a question of trying to get them to learn each other's good qualities and to recognise their own bad qualities. I can't say it's something I've found easy to do. Sometimes it works and sometimes it doesn't. We had a big management shakeup in BHS when I could see that certain people were just not going to change their spots. Although they were perfectly competent people and good at their jobs, they were never going to become part of the new culture which we have been trying to design for the Storehouse group. So they left the business.
>
> I find that a very difficult situation, because I can see the merits in most people. Most senior executives in a business have got plenty of good qualities. The problem is assessing whether they are going to change or not and I suppose I get criticised for being too tolerant at times. I like to give people a very fair chance. When people seem to be falling down, I like to give them the opportunity to

right themselves. If they can't do that they simply have to go. I certainly wouldn't go into a new business and make instant decisions about who has got to go. I would try and get people to work as a team together and then when it obviously isn't going to work properly, only then would I make the decision. Some people probably think I take too long to decide such matters, but I can demonstrate to them that sometimes by giving people a reasonable length of time to adjust they come through with flying colours.

I particularly try and develop an atmosphere of autonomy in the subsidiary companies where they feel they are part of a team and can look across at the other companies and can see admirable things going on. It's a rather bad analogy, but I like to think of them as first-division football teams with their own particular qualities. You let them play against one another and sometimes you transfer a player from one club to another, so that it builds up a mutual admiration society.

Conran is first and foremost an entrepreneur, who lives up magnificently to his own definition of what such a person should be: someone who takes risks after carefully assessing the opportunities available to him. He does not believe that Britain lacks for entrepreneurs, but he is concerned that many of them do not do their homework well enough.

I remember once being on the board of a risk capital company when the Business Expansion Scheme first came in. There were hundreds of companies coming to us for funds and they were meant to be writing their business plans properly and cogently. I was absolutely horrified at the number of flaws you could very quickly find in reading one of these papers for half an hour. Their thinking was coloured about how they were going to make their million and be launched on the USM. They were all aspiring entrepreneurs, but so few of them had an original idea. I think the most important thing is to try and find that gap in the market that is not well trodden by a lot of other people – to find something which you can do which is different from all the rest of them.

> There's no point in just joining a mass of people who are simply competing with one another. One of the reasons we developed a design-led retail business, offering our own unique products, was because we saw we could distance ourselves from other retailers who were just selling manufacturers' products and discounting them and getting into constant competitive battles. It's difficult to be an entrepreneur, I believe, by simply following a well-trodden path.

Conran never really switches off from work, because he surrounds himself by objects that are beautifully designed. He drives a Porsche, because apart from being a car that operates in harmony with man, in Conran's view, it is also beautiful to behold. 'I've always driven a Porsche ever since I could afford one. I'm one of the original Yuppies, I suppose. It's a beautiful car, beautifully engineered and a great pleasure to drive. The actual process of driving yourself in a Porsche makes you feel good.'

His main hobby is to take derelict old buildings and convert them into habitable homes that are monuments to the Conran design credo. He has two such homes in France, one in Provence, which he visits frequently. He has recently completed a book on all the aspects of France he loves so much. In the heart of the English countryside he runs a workshop where four craftsmen turn out fine furniture. It is a hobby he has taken up with two main aims in mind: 'Firstly, it keeps my hand in as far as manufacturing is concerned and secondly I like to see this small bit of entrepreneuralism on my doorstep. I find it very relaxing.'

Conran doesn't see anything ostentatious about owning four homes.

> I have to have a home in London because I live and work here. I like being in the country very much indeed. My real home is in the country near Hungerford. I love being in France and I recently bought an old barn there and took great pleasure in rebuilding it and making a garden. It's not essential for me to have four houses. In many ways I would prefer to live in one place, but taking old and derelict houses and making them relive again is a source of enjoyment to me.

Although Conran is very conscious of what he buys and surrounds himself with, he has not allowed his love of good design to become a fetish. He applies the same pragmatic attitude to design in his leisure-time pursuits as he does to the working environment. For example, he does not seek out chic restaurants that are the haunt of the artistic set. He is more likely to enjoy going to a restaurant that has good traditional furnishings that are well designed in their own terms.

> What I am anxious to do is to find things that are not cynically made. It is the cynicism in the design process that offends me; the suggestion that there's no point in designing anything special for the working classes because they don't have any taste. People's taste is created not by their genes but by what they're offered in the shops. If they're offered, as they have been for years and years ever since the industrial revolution, things that have been cynically designed for the working classes, is it surprising that we have a nation of people who are supposed to have no visual standards? It is only when people are shown and offered things that excite their brains and imagination that standards go up. When the British started to go out of Britain and go abroad for their holidays their eyes were opened. They started to eat different food, see different clothes and furniture in the shops and different houses and their perspective widened.

Sir John Cuckney

Born: Murree, India, 1925.
Educated: Shrewsbury; St Andrew's University.

Sir John Cuckney is chairman of 3i Group plc and Royal Insurance plc and a former chairman of Westland Group plc; deputy chairman of TI Group plc; a director of Brixton Estate plc and a former director of Midland Bank plc.

After service with the Royal Northumberland Fusiliers in World War II, he was attached to the War Office until 1957. Since then he has held directorships of various industrial and financial companies, including Standard Industrial Group (director 1959–66, managing director 1966–70), Standard Industrial Trust (chairman 1966–70) and Lazard Bros & Company (currently a member of the board).

He was chairman of Brooke Bond Group plc from 1981 to 1984; chairman of John Brown plc from 1983 to 1986 and chairman of Thomas Cook Group Ltd from 1978 to 1987.

In the public sector, he was chairman of the Mersey Docks and Harbour Board (1970–72); the Port of London Authority (1977–79); the Building Economic Development Committee (Little Neddy) (1976–80) and International Military Services Ltd (owned by the Ministry of Defence) from 1974 to 1985.

In 1972 he was appointed chief executive (second permanent secretary) to set up the Property Services Agency at the Department of the Environment and held that position until his appointment as chairman of the Crown Agents for Overseas Governments and Administrations in 1974, which he held until 1978. He was chairman of the International Maritime Bureau (of the International Chamber of Commerce) from 1981 to 1985.

He is a freeman of the City of London. He received his knighthood in the 1978 Birthday Honours List and in 1980

SIR JOHN CUCKNEY

was elected an Elder Brother and a Member of the Court of Trinity House.

Sir John Cuckney's career has embraced a fascinating mix of public- and private-sector service, a combination he has always found very appealing. Even after deciding to put public service behind him and concentrate on the private sector, he has never quite seemed able to escape involvement with government. A classic example was when he found himself at the centre of media and national attention after taking over the chairmanship of the troubled Westland Group in June 1985. He set about drawing up a rescue plan amid a political storm that resulted in the resignation of two cabinet ministers.

But possibly because of his broad experience of both the public and private sectors, Cuckney rode out the storm calmly. Once the Prime Minister had declared that Westland's problems were a private-sector matter and not something that should be unduly influenced by government issues, his priorities became abundantly clear.

Cuckney's longest stint in government service lasted for about ten years. After World War II, during which he served in the army with the Royal Northumberland Fusiliers, he was attached to the War Office. But by 1957 he had become disenchanted with government service and decided it was time to join the private sector. 'In the mid-1950s I found public service very restrictive. I wanted the greater freedom which obtains in the private sector.'

He went to work for an organisation that combined the roles of an issuing house and a conglomerate. The two sides of the business were interrelated and operated in parallel. The issuing house was active in turning small- and medium-sized firms into public companies. At the same time, an industrial holding company was being built up by acquiring firms which, for various reasons, were unsuitable for turning into public companies.

In 1970 an opportunity came Cuckney's way which offered the kind of unusual challenge he has always relished. He was invited to become chairman of the Mersey Docks and Harbour Board, which fell into the grey area between the public and private sector for which Sir John has always found special fascination.

It also faced him with the need to untangle a financial crisis, a task that has frequently occupied him in his career.

> It was an interesting problem. The Mersey Docks and Harbour Board was a public-trust authority which was becoming rapidly insolvent, yet there was no way in law in which it could go into liquidation. The only type of receiver who could be appointed was a receiver of rates who has no control over assets and no management control which a receiver normally has.
>
> It had an active business operation side and Seaforth – the container port – was still being built. So it presented a mix of business operations of a rather specialised type, but also a classic area of interface between the public and private sector. As a public-trust authority with central government funds committed to it through the Harbour Act, it needed a private bill to get its constitution altered. So there was a parliamentary battle. It was a mix of problems that I very much like.

After this, Cuckney again found himself drawn to public service. he became a second permanent secretary in the Department of the Environment during Edward Heath's administration. His somewhat thankless task was to attempt to introduce private-sector techniques into the Civil Service by setting up the Property Services Agency.

> It had a very ill-fated start in that some of the original ideas of establishing it as an independent agency with a trading fund were thwarted at the last moment. It remained an integral part of a government department but with an attempt to try to introduce accountable management and run it in a businesslike fashion. It was called a departmental agency, but the constraints of trying to be fully integrated with a major department like the Department of the Environment meant that the theoretical freedom to manage, which it had started off with, very quickly disappeared.

After two years, Cuckney left to become chairman of the Crown Agents, another organisation that was encountering fairly major financial difficulties. And again, it was an organisation with a blurred constitution.

> Central government's responsibility for it was not at all clear. It moved into banking and property development just ahead of the secondary banking crisis. It was still fulfilling its traditional functions of looking after overseas governments and acting as a purchasing agency for them – and indeed it did administer World Bank and British Government overseas development loans.

It took Cuckney four years to overcome the financial crisis he encountered when he took over the Crown Agents in 1974. Towards the end of this period he also became chairman of the Port of London Authority. But by the latter part of the 1970s he experienced an irresistible urge to return to the private sector and he had a very clear idea of how he would go about it.

> Going back into the private sector I was very keen to become a pluralist. I didn't want to be totally dependent on any one source of income or any one group. I think the most attractive feature of being a pluralist is the independence it gives and that has certainly been borne out in my experience. I very deliberately wanted a mix of interests.

On leaving the Crown Agents he became a director of Midland Bank and chairman of Thomas Cook, which Midland Bank owned, and he became a director and subsequently chairman of Brooke Bond and a director and subsequently chairman of Royal Insurance.

After eight years in the public sector, Cuckney was more than ready to become involved with private industry, but he firmly believes more top executives in the UK ought to join the traffic between the two sectors. 'The movement you often see exhibited in France where people move very frequently from the public to the private sector and back again is something which I wish happened more often here.'

But Cuckney does not find it easy to put his finger on the

fundamental differences between operating in the two sectors.

> There are, of course, differences and I've often wondered what is the most significant difference. As a permanent secretary in the Department of the Environment I was an accounting officer, which meant as a civil servant I was responsible directly to parliament, which also meant I regularly had to go before the Public Accounts Committee. Shortly after I left the public sector again, I was invited to chair a seminar at the Civil Service Staff College at Sunningdale comparing being an accounting officer in the Civil Service and being chairman of a public company and appearing before an annual general meeting. It was a very interesting comparison one was forced to make.
>
> The most fundamental difference to me has always been that the private sector is so much more dynamic – the rate of change is so great. Of course, there are changes in the public sector, changes in organisation – indeed government finds it an almost irresistible temptation to tinker with its machinery, merge departments, break them up and give them new titles. But despite all that, there is a great solidity; there is a great security-cum-fairly rigid structure supporting the Civil Service – and necessarily so. It needs to have continuity and stability but in the private sector the real difference is the incredible rate of change in the market place. The external factors affecting your business are constantly changing and you have in order to survive to adapt to these external changes. It's a nice idea that in business or banking you can go through a period of 'consolidation', but it seldom works out that way.

The more dynamic pace of change in the private sector is something that appeals to Cuckney.

> I like the challenge that you've got to identify changes in the externals and you need to take initiatives. Nobody is going to tell you what to do. You've got to make your own judgements and assessments. If you are involved in a business with overseas investments – and more and more businesses have to think in global market terms – you need

to be conscious of the very rapidly changing international scene. The international political and economical scene is rarely stable. If you're interested in current affairs, as I am, they have a very direct impact on your business.

It was perhaps ironic that having decided to dedicate the rest of his career to the private sector that Cuckney became caught up in a major government row when he took over as chairman of Westland Group. The UK's only helicopter manufacturer was on the brink of insolvency. There was a shortfall in orders to carry the company into the 1990s – the famous 'black hole' – and it was vastly overmanned for the amount of work that was likely to come its way in the immediate future. In 1985 Westland was making losses of £95m on a turnover of £308m and its future looked bleak. Quite clearly, an urgent rescue plan was needed.

At one point it looked as though the helicopter operator and entrepreneur Alan Bristow would come to the company's rescue, but when he changed his mind there was a crisis of confidence. Westland became the centre of a political storm between Michael Heseltine, then Defence Minister, and Leon Brittan, Secretary of State for Trade and Industry, over the form the rescue package should take. Heseltine was anxious to set up a link between Westland and a consortium of European helicopter companies, whereas the DTI was adamant the company should make up its own mind. There was a lot of emotive talk about the UK's only helicopter company selling out to the Americans, but in the event the Sikorsky-Fiat minority involvement won the day and Heseltine resigned from the government.

The political storm disguised the fundamental problems facing Westland which Cuckney, as chairman, and chief executive Hugh Stewart set about tackling. The work-force was pruned by two thousand people and a new management structure was introduced to reduce Westland's dependence on helicopter sales and place greater emphasis on new technologies and components for the aerospace industry.

In hindsight, it's difficult to understand what all the furore was about, since Sikorsky only took a minority stake in Westland, but at the height of the storm Cuckney found himself in the unwelcome glare of national publicity. It's an experience he is glad to put behind him.

Westland was a unique situation, hopefully never to be repeated. One began recognising at the outset, of course, that there was an important relationship to government in that government was the main customer, the main purchaser of the product. One also had links with government to the extent that the DTI provided launch aid for civil helicopter developments and the Ministry of Defence part-financed development aid for helicopters, or improvements to them, for defence purposes. So one started at Westland knowing you were going to have two major government involvements. When you're in a defence industry that is inevitable. There were fundamental differences between these two government departments – between two ministers – and Westland was piggy-in-the-middle, which was a very costly and unfortunate experience.

The important issue for me as chairman throughout that period was to remember that once the Prime Minister had said that Westland was a private-sector problem which must be solved by private-sector measures and techniques, one's interests were obviously the shareholders, the employees, the customers and the banks, since the company was heavily indebted. One was not then justified in thinking and functioning in terms of what might be in the national interest, what might ultimately be a desirable development for NATO strategy or defence strategy. It was rather a more specific and harsher problem which, to put it bluntly, was to survive as Westland was drifting on to the rocks of insolvency.

We knew in 1985 that when we made our preliminary announcement of our results for the previous financial year that we would become technically insolvent. So the main thrust of all one's efforts was to try and save the company as a corporate entity and secure the interests of the employees, the shareholders and the banks.

Confining his attention to private-sector issues, Cuckney was in no doubt about what his priorities were. Divorced of all the political drama, the issue was reasonably straightforward – which rescue plan offered Westland the best prospects of survival? It was of little consequence which quarter it came from.

There was a lot of misunderstanding about the European-American argument. As far as the company was concerned, as one drifted nearer to insolvency, any rescuer who appeared would have been welcome provided we'd been absolutely assured at the critical time when the loss of £92m was announced that a rescue was legally binding, underwritten and in place.

What was attractive about the American consortium approach – and I must emphasise that it was never a take-over bid, Sikorsky's stake is only eight per cent – was firstly, we had worked with Sikorsky on and off for forty years. But of overriding importance was the sheer professionalism of the American participation. United Technologies (Sikorsky's parent group) came to take part in what developed into a contested capital reconstruction with a proxy battle. They came armed with batteries of attorneys, British and American, merchant bank and investment bank advisers and the way in which their participation developed was immensely thorough. One had greater faith on the day that one would be assured of their support – and incidentally the negotiations with the banks were fairly difficult.

The European consortium did not appear to us to be particularly cohesive in their aims and objectives. It was less clear what their ultimate intentions were for the company. One had a fairly strong feeling that part of their motivation was negative, in that it was to exclude the American participation, rather than positive – to build up the company.

The experience underlined for Cuckney the importance of having clear goals in a crisis and being determined not to waver from the chosen course of action:

I think you have to be extremely clear-minded and unemotional about what your objectives are and if it is a public company you must remember the paramount importance of the owners of the business – the shareholders. I had, as it happens, had experience just before Westland of another very well-known public company – John Brown – which had encountered difficulties. As chairman, I had been involved in its capital reconstruction and ultimate sale to

Trafalgar House. What was interesting about that was that at the time John Brown got into financial difficulties the banks and institutional shareholders took a tough but very constructive view that it was worth helping the company through a reconstruction rather than forcing it into liquidation, which had been an attitude prevalent some years earlier.

It was in fact my experience of working with the banks and institutions for the recapitalisation and reconstruction of John Brown which led me to think that the City is much maligned over its attitudes to industry and the accusation of short-termism is not justified. The institutions and banks had been immensely supportive in helping save the company. When I was approached over Westland, it was by some of the banks and institutions that had been involved in the John Brown affair. One of my reasons for becoming involved in Westland was that I felt in some respects that I owed them something.

Cuckney has never found it difficult switching from the public to the private sector, or vice versa. He has found the management problems in each sector to be remarkably similar. 'There is a lot of common ground – the same causes for companies and organisations encountering difficulties, but of course the solutions have to be tailor-made to a particular industry or company culture.'

A sound organisation structure helps to overcome many operational problems, in Cuckney's view.

It is extremely important that you have an organisation structure that is clearly understood and then you should not keep altering it. That can be very destructive. But I think you have to recognise that there is no ideal organisation structure, whatever the arguments are for centralisation, decentralisation, functionalisation, regionalisation, for a line-management or matrix-management approach. What really matters are the personal relationships within the structure. There will always be imperfections and they can only be overcome by personal relationships.

I think there are enough common factors in management, including the role of chairman, that apply to all or most businesses, such as the need for careful succession planning,

> the need for developing a strategy or a corporate plan. When I say corporate plan, I don't necessarily mean you have to live with it rigidly. Putting it at its simplest it should be at least a clear mission statement which the whole organisation understands. I also think that apart from the corporate plan, the strategy and the mission statement, you really do need to give some vision about the future of your company and a vision in which those working with you can share. You can usually tell an organisation that has a clear corporate plan but very little vision about the future. The lack of vision is reflected in the atmosphere among the staff and all the employees.

Cuckney also feels that a top executive needs to set an example by being something of an entrepreneurial risk-taker.

> There's a need for an entrepreneurial spirit. After all, in the whole of the private sector there is a need for innovation; there is a need sometimes for diversification, although that can be a dangerous area; there is a need for a sensitive but effective response to the changing market place. All of that is going to involve risk-taking.

Cuckney does not believe that the qualities needed to be an effective chairman of a financial institution such as 3i (Investors in Industry) are that different to those required to oversee a manufacturing company. He is not even convinced that the head of a financial institution needs to be all that numerate.

> I think the really critical issue is to understand the concepts behind the particular forms of financing which are used. People do tend, I think rather superficially, to concentrate on figures and relationships between the figures, whereas what really matters is the concept behind them and I think a financier could be somebody who is awfully bad at arithmetic, but does understand the concepts.

Cuckney is chairman of 3i, which claims to be the largest venture-capital organisation in the world. It was established in 1945 as the Industrial, Commercial and Financial Corporation to try to ensure that British industry had access to sufficient funds to feed its long-term growth. Using funds raised in public capital markets all over the world, 3i is a major force in the provision of share and loan capital to unquoted British companies. Owned since its formation by the clearing banks (eighty-five per cent) and the Bank of England (fifteen per cent), it represents a commercially successful, City-based initiative to help meet British industry's long-term capital requirements. Since 1945, 3i has supported over nine thousand companies. It provided over £500m in capital in 1987 to nine hundred businesses.

It invests in all the major points of change in the life of a company, from start-ups through to flotation. In a typical year it supports some three hundred brand new or very young ventures. Its total assets are over £2bn.

> What 3i has done is demonstrate that the clearing banks in the UK have collectively over forty years ensured that there is access to long-term development capital for British industry. It is a living example which shows that the accusations of short-termism levelled against the City are really not valid – certainly in this respect. What has been achieved by 3i over the years is a very clear demonstration that the banking system has done a lot to help the growth of small and medium-sized businesses.

Cuckney challenges the view that there are vast sums of money locked up in pension funds floating around the City that could be diverted towards helping struggling small firms to grow.

> I don't think the market place is ill-organised. I don't think there is any shortage of venture capital or money to back good propositions. What there is a shortage of is good propositions which are realistically priced and properly thought through and presented.

The 3i chairman is convinced that an enterprise economy does now genuinely exist in Britain.

> One can see it by the numbers of new business start-ups; also by the number of failures which does show there is

> some healthy risk-taking. I think one sees it by the change in the structure of big business, by so many management buy-outs and the realisation that size is not everything; large companies concentrating more on their core businesses and getting rid of peripheral businesses and spending more on research and development in supporting core businesses. I think there is a dynamic movement in the structure of industry and in the geographic location of industry, the move away from some of the old traditional steel and coal mining and heavy industries into service industries and electronics, which does very clearly demonstrate that an enterprise economy does now exist.

Cuckney was attracted to the chairmanship of 3i because it is an organisation that has an interesting mix of expertise,

> not only of financially trained and financially innovative people, but it also has a strong contingent of industrial advisers. It's an organisation I have always recognised provides a facility to commerce and industry which I think is highly desirable – that is a facility to take a long-term view. It's an essential feature of 3i that the positions it takes are long term. It has been a shareholder for a very long time in some private companies and I think we've become known to be a supportive shareholder. We certainly were with British Caledonian.

More recently 3i has become involved in the fashionable technique of 'buy-ins', where teams of successful managers are headhunted from larger companies to run smaller struggling firms and turn then around. Cuckney regards such managerial mobility as healthy.

> I see no objections at all to it. I think the development of buy-ins and management buy-outs, spin-outs, and all that kind of thing are a good indication of adjustment and adaptation to changes in industry. One of the factors common to businesses that have fallen on hard times is an inability to adapt and change and a failure to recognise that the market place is changing around them. I think there is

always going to be this element in business. It's rather like pond life – little tadpoles eating even smaller ones and bigger ones eating them. I think that movement is essential.

One of the major changes industry had to adapt to in the autumn of 1987 was the stock-market slump that sent share prices plummeting. Cuckney does not believe the crash was the result of any fundamental change in the structure of national economies, but he does suggest that it signals the fact that greater volatility in global markets is here to stay.

I think we in Europe have been a bit slow to recognise that we are in a totally new era. With all the new techniques now available, such as twenty-four hour trading and the global marketing of securities, we have been a bit slow to adapt to changes that are now going to be permanent. A domestic market that becomes part of an international market is going to be subjected to the effects of changes which might otherwise have been more slow in coming – or wouldn't have immediately affected it.

All this has coincided perhaps with some inevitable over-optimism. There have been some rather unrealistic valuations being put on businesses. But I think the critical issue of Black Monday and what's happened since is that this is a very major change in the nature of the market place, but not in the underlying economies of countries, especially the UK. I think we will continue to have a degree of volatility in markets we've not experienced previously and I think the way the market maker has to interpret his role now is such that we will never get the sort of fine tuning that the old jobbing system could provide.

With so much more volatility in markets, it is perhaps inevitable that greater stress will be put on senior executives as they strive to adapt to, and cope with, ever faster changes. The ability to deal with crisis is something Cuckney has cultivated over the years.

During the Westland episode my worry beads got red hot on occasions, but I think each time you go through a corporate crisis of some sort, you'd be silly if you haven't learned from the previous ones. I think it's terribly important in an organisational crisis to remember that the crisis aspect of it, the critical nature of it, is something you've got to put to one side. You've got to get on and deal with the problem and forget it's a crisis. I think if you don't do that, you'll very easily become over-influenced at the time by the fact that it is a crisis you're dealing with. You should treat it as a straightforward job of work and get on with it.

In any crisis, my greatest support is a clean sheet of paper and a pencil and the telephone off the hook. I think it is absolutely essential that you are extremely clear-minded on your objectives and you're extremely clear-minded on your order of priorities, remembering the prime aim is to serve the shareholders and their interests.

Sir Monty Finniston

Born: Glasgow, 1912.
Educated: University of Strathclyde (formerly the Royal College of Science and Technology).

Sir Monty Finniston is a former chairman of the British Steel Corporation and now runs his own company, H.M. Finniston, in London.

He began his business career in 1948 when he became chief metallurgist at the United Kingdom Atomic Energy Authority at Harwell. In January 1959 he joined C.A. Parsons as managing director of its subsidiary, International Research and Development Company, the largest sponsored research organisation in the UK. He was chairman of the organisation from 1968 to 1977.

In 1967 he was appointed deputy chairman of the nationalised British Steel Corporation and in 1971 took on the additional responsibility of chief executive. He relinquished both posts in 1973 when he became chairman of the corporation for a period of three years.

In 1976 he joined Sears Holdings Ltd as a director and Sears Engineering Ltd as chairman. He resigned from Sears in October 1979 prior to setting up his own company in 1980.

He is chairman of a number of companies, including K.C.A. Drilling plc, Sherwood International Ltd, Industrial Technology Securities Ltd, and Mullholland Ltd. His directorships include that of Cluff Oil plc, British Nutrition Foundation, Caledonian Heritable Estates and Combined Capital Ltd.

He is chairman of the Council of the Scottish Business School, the Prison Reform Trust and the Scottish Enterprise Foundation.

He is president of a number of business-related associations, including the Industrial Building Bureau, the Industrial Marketing Research Association, the Institute of Mechanical & General

Technician Engineers, the Engineering Industries Association, the British Export Houses Association and the Society of Environmental Engineers.

He is chancellor of Stirling University and a freeman of the City of London.

Sir Monty Finniston entered the industrial arena relatively late in life. He was already fifty-five years old when he took up his first corporate post, as technical director of C.A. Parsons, manufacturers of electrical generators, transformers and turbines. A research scientist by profession and temperament, he had spent all his previous career 'never more than ten yards away from a laboratory'.

Once he had made the switch, however, Finniston tackled his successive responsibilities with great relish, including the awesome task of reorganising the British Steel Corporation, which at the time was 260,000 strong. Stark though the contrast must have been, Sir Monty explains the transfer from the closeted laboratory life to the public glare of big business with simple logic:

> I didn't think I was being very original any longer and I was basically administering. If you're administering, you might as well administer something that is new and challenging rather than doing something I had been doing all my life. It happens to many scientists.

His first challenge was to take charge of a nuclear research centre for C.A. Parsons, which at the time employed 350 graduates and trained scientists, but for which there was little work. Finniston converted it into a major international research organisation that still exists today. But his horizons were dramatically broadened when he joined British Steel and was asked by the late Lord Melchett, who was then chairman, to reorganise the fourteen widely dispersed companies that had been put into the same melting pot under the nationalisation programme.

It took Finniston a year to complete the task.

> That taught me a lot about how you actually get people to

operate within a hierarchical structure. It was a fundamental reorganisation, because fourteen private companies working in rivalry with one another is quite a different thing from fourteen companies being merged into a single corporation with a single objective.

The experience caused Finniston to do some thinking about people and their relationship to organisations. McKinsey, the leading management consulting group, which advised on the restructuring, held the firm view that people should always fulfil the specifications of the job. It rejected any idea that an organisation should ever be created to suit the individual characteristics of people. Finniston questions whether this approach can be adopted slavishly.

This philosophy obviously works in some cases when it is an established function like an accountant. But on many occasions you've got talented people who just don't fill the job specifications, but whose qualities, put to an objective agreed by everybody, are valuable beyond measure.

After completing the restructuring of British Steel, Finniston was asked to draw up the group's first corporate plan. It formed the basis of the ten-year development programme that was submitted to the government in 1973. The project involved an in-depth analysis of British Steel's operating units to examine how they stood against international competition. Finniston made some startling discoveries.

When I joined the company it had fifty-eight blast furnaces, the largest of which produced 2,750 tons a day. The smallest blast furnace the Japanese were building then produced 10,000 tons a day. So we had to make radical changes. We didn't need fifty-eight blast furnaces. It only called for eight at the most.

It was a mammoth task, but Finniston considers that his scientific background fitted him well for the challenge.

Scientific training makes you think rationally and logically.

To start with you have to deal with every problem rationally. That forms the basis of your planning. Then you have to say that, of course, the world is not a rational place. It's got all kinds of people and all kinds of situations you didn't take into account and you couldn't take into account. The money you have at your disposal, for example. To do the task requires X amount of pounds, but you've only got X minus something. Then you have to modify the base to suit particular circumstances.

The implementation of the rationalisation programme left a lasting impression on Finniston which was to influence his future operating style. The original 260,000 employees have since been whittled down to 50,000 and Sir Monty is a little resentful that he is probably most remembered for setting that radical rundown in motion. His was not an enviable duty.

In rationalising the corporation and giving it the equipment that would allow it to compete with rivals, particularly foreign rivals, I had to have a capital programme. The capital programme, as in all manufacturing industries, required a reduction in manpower. Productivity had to go up and this was going to be achieved through the introduction of new capital rather than the introduction of new labour.

I became chief executive in 1971 and I then became responsible for the implementation of the plan. It was quite clear to me that 260,000 people would be reduced very substantially and that for every person who was made redundant in British Steel, seven people were affected – another three in the family, plus the people serving that family in the shops and in other ways.

Finniston pauses for an ironical chuckle as he recollects the weight of responsibility placed upon his shoulders at the time. 'So there I was, responsible for nearly two million people in a way. That's a big chunk of the population and I worried about the hardship that I was causing as a result of what was really a commercial decision.'

He first began to think about the repercussions of such hard commercial decisions in 1971, and by the time that he became chairman of British Steel upon the untimely death of Lord Melchett he had formulated a way to ease the hardship. He set up an organisation called BSC Industry, which had the prime task of counselling redundant steel workers, retraining them and helping them to redirect their careers and, in many instances, set up their own small businesses. It was a positive answer to an appalling problem that has since been copied in different forms by many other industries. At the time it was revolutionary approach. Finniston proudly describes it 'as the first essay in caring capitalism that I know of.'

'If you take Ebbw Vale as an example, where we rendered 2,500 people redundant in a very close community, we got 1,500 people back to work again within eighteen months by the start-up of nineteen companies. We did that without any financial help from the government of the day.'

The experience made Finniston aware of the needs of people when making major corporate decisions.

> I became very much more conscious of people, because when you're a scientist you're dealing with inanimate matter, unless you're a biologist. Inanimate matter doesn't answer back and if you get fed up with what you're doing you throw it down the sink or get rid of it. But you can't do that with people. They are the only appreciating asset you have in business. All the other assets disappear; you write them off. You depreciate them every year. In five years a machine is counted as nothing in the balance sheet, but people count and age makes them more experienced, gives them better judgement – if they're capable of learning, which most people are.

In addition to the people aspects of a business, Finniston also had to pick up fairly swiftly a keen understanding of commercial factors, such as pricing. He dismisses the popular theory of the need to price according to what the market will bear.

> That's a stupid phrase actually. How do you know what the market will bear? Do you hold a wet finger up to the wind and say that's it or do you calculate what it is? There are many difficult commercial decisions. How much do you

produce in advance? How can you gauge what a market's worth? Never mind the home market, what about the foreign market? How do you go into competition with people? How do you get over protectionism?

Finniston admits that being plunged into the deep end of commercial decisions he inevitably made mistakes in the early stages, although he is not prepared to take the blame entirely. 'If the mistakes had been that obvious there were people around me to tell me where I had gone wrong, but they didn't. So perhaps they would have made the same mistakes as well.'

He believes his most serious mistake was wanting to get things done in a hurry. In hindsight he wishes he had been more patient, particularly with the twenty-nine different unions he had to deal with at British Steel.

I tried to get the trade unions into a form which made my managerial activities easier rather than trying to let them find a consensus between themselves. But I was in a hurry to get things done. I think patience is very important, particularly with people. Of course it conflicts with the commercial urgency of producing something or gaining a new market. You've got to balance the urgency of the situation against the patience required to do it.

Finniston is in no doubt that making decisions and seeing them implemented properly are the most important aspects of a chairman's job. He was once asked what he considered the function of a chairman to be and he gave a three-part answer:

First the chairman must be quite clear what the objectives of the company are. It doesn't matter what size the company is, whether it's in manufacturing or services. He's got to say this is what he's trying to do in order to gain what it is he's trying to gain. The objectives must be quite clear. Every year after I became chairman of British Steel we set aside one board meeting at which the objectives of the organisation were raised. We never changed them very much, because we knew the path we were on, but we consciously spoke about them.

> Secondly, having decided the objective, make quite sure you've got the resources to meet it – that means in man-power, money, in machines and in markets. There's no point in idealising a policy and never being in a position to achieve it. It's much better in those circumstances to reduce the objective. Then thirdly, make quite sure the objective is implemented properly, so you have to monitor. You don't monitor day in and day out, hanging over the shoulders of individuals but periodically you go in and question why people are not meeting deadlines they've agreed to.

Finniston also believes that choosing a good successor is an important duty of a chairman, but as chairman of a nationalised industry he was in no position to do so.

The former steel boss recalls that he was able to assimilate the theoretical aspects of senior management very quickly and implement them in an almost academic fashion. But he found there was nothing academic about dealing with people and with the unions, because 'established institutions have their dogmas and their attitudes are frozen rigid.'

He picked up a few tricks of the trade as he progressed.

> In union negotiations, for example, I always found that if you had a heart to heart with the opposition, the single leader, you could probably gain something. At some stage, informal contacts can be very effective. They can't be informal to start with. People have got to define where they stand – on both sides.

A case in point was a series of devastating strikes that Finniston had to weather at British Steel in 1974. The corporation was sustaining appalling production losses and Finniston wrote to each of the trade unions suggesting that they meet on the neutral territory of a Heathrow hotel. He gave the union leaders the opportunity to tell him in a forthright manner where they thought he was going wrong with his policies and he in turn did some pretty plain talking about what he saw as their shortcomings. The idea was so successful in defusing the explosive situation that the meetings continued to be held at six-monthly intervals.

The special relationship Finniston forged between top management and the work-force at British Steel is epitomised by the fact that he was given farewell parties by each of the seven major steelworks when he came to leave the corporation at the end of ten years. That was something he took great pride in.

In many respects, Finniston was ahead of his time in the management policies he adopted during the period he was chairman of British Steel but he stresses that commercial strategy without enlightened personnel policies can never be successful.

> I don't think if you just consider products or a market in the abstract that you can be ahead of your time. That's not the kind of vision that distinguishes people. It's when at the end of your career you can say that you have benefitted some part of society, if not all of society, that you can say you have done well.

Finniston's greatest disappointment during his time at British Steel was that he never succeeded in persuading the unions to form a single group to simplify negotiations. 'It made it unnecessarily complex having to deal with so many.' But he was never overawed by the sheer scale of the task he undertook. 'That never worried me. I've never worried about large orders of magnitude. Problem solving is quite independent of the magnitude of the figures. It just means you have to think more carefully, that's all.'

Creativity is an essential prerequisite of running a company successfully, in Finniston's estimation, and in 1978 he outlined the elements of creative management to a gathering of The Royal Society of Arts. It would be hard to improve on his observations today:

> Creative management is about creative managers. What then makes a creative manager? Basically, he must be endowed with or develop certain characteristics of character. He must have the will to engage in management as a changing, improving exercise benefitting his company, those responsible to him and for him.
>
> He must have *courage* since there will be many obstacles to the achievement of his objectives.

He must be *resilient* since he must recover when there are setbacks.

He must be *patient* since there is no instant creativity and implementation takes time.

He must be *critical of himself* – and others – since in a changing world he must constantly be questioning his methods, his direction and the administration of his responsibilities.

He must be *thoughtful* since lack of thought is probably responsible for most of the world's difficulties.

He must be *communicative* since he has to work with or through other people.

He must be *educated* with professional expertise, not just in a specialist discipline but with a general knowledge of the disciplines which bear on management, to allow communication with other contributors to the industrial activity of the company or organisation.

He must *learn to delegate*, encouraging those responsible to him by placing responsibility and authority on them as part of their career education.

And he must be *aware of people* since he is not only concerned with the technical standing of machines but also with the physical and mental health of his operators.

The paragon of all these virtues is a rare animal – but thankfully is not extinct and hopefully will continue to breed.

Finniston still puts great store in these qualities today and he believes they equally apply to any kind of company or organisation.

I don't think what you run makes any difference, because I've run companies of very diverse natures and the principles that apply to British Steel at one end apply equally to a small company at the other end of the scale. What I would most strongly suggest as the conditioning factor is the people you have to work with. This determines everything. That's why you can have two people who are going to occupy the same position and you'll treat them quite differently, because of the different characters. There are some people who know best all the time. They may have other qualities which are worthwhile having, but trying to get them to change their minds requires one kind of approach. There are other people who only work by consensus, but once they've agreed to something they'll do it very effectively. That requires a different approach. Finding people and educating and training them without them being aware that it's being done is very important.

The former steel boss takes the view that any intelligent manager can learn the technicalities of a new industry reasonably quickly. It didn't take him long to master the basics of what British Steel was all about and he has been just as versatile in acquiring an understanding of a diverse range of other businesses, from computers and oil drilling to knitwear machines. The art, according to Finniston, is to ask intelligent questions and look for inconsistencies. By phrasing questions in different ways, inconsistencies are exposed without the need for having a detailed knowledge of a particular technique.

There is one area of management, however, that Sir Monty has changed his view on as a result of greater experience.

I used to believe it was possible to make forecasts – market forecasts in particular – which were likely to be accurate. I no longer believe solely in figures. I believe in sensitivity analyses and I believe in ranges. But I've come to the conclusion that these are sometimes a bit astrological, particularly if you're in a competitive situation. You've got to know what your rivals are doing.

Finniston cites Japan as a vivid example.

I know Japan is the country everyone points to, but it is the favourite one because it happens to show all the deficiencies of forecasting and combatting rivalry that are available. In 1951 the Japanese produced only 6 million tons of steel and in that same year the British steel industry produced 15 million tons. In 1981 – thirty years later – the Japanese were producing over 100 million tons and we were still producing only 15 million tons. You've got to ask yourself what they had that we didn't have. Or what did they do we should have done? It wasn't because we didn't have the talent. It's not because we couldn't have done it. The country didn't have the will to do it and the politicians didn't have the will to do it.

Finniston firmly believes that a lack of training and inadequate educational facilities are two of the major stumbling blocks to industrial efficiency in Britain. He cites some statistics from two recent reports to support his argument:

> Of all the people who call themselves managers or are designated managers in Japan or the US, eighty-five per cent have a degree qualification. The figure in this country is twenty-four per cent. In the US, West Germany and Japan five full days every year are devoted to off-the-job training for every manager. In this country it's less than one day. Now I'm quite happy to argue we're twice as good as the Japanese, but I'm not prepared to claim we're four times as good, which is what these figures suggest.

Finniston also believes that there should be a greater element of entrepreneurship in all types of businesses. He points out wryly that 'entrepreneur' is a French term and that there is no equivalent word in the English language. A literal translation would be 'undertaker', which doesn't have quite the right ring! He contends that the whole of the business world is,

> a risk-taking business. The term, enterprise, really is a four-letter word – RISK. But we play safe. Take this craze for making everyone a shareholder. The bulk of investors put money into gilts. But putting money into small new firms, where the failure rate is pretty high and great risks are being taken, that's what enterprise is all about.

Today, Finniston runs his own small firm (small by comparison with British Steel at any rate), but at least fifty per cent of his time is now taken up with interests outside the corporate world. He is chancellor of Stirling University and spends a lot of time going around lecturing at universities and schools. He has been chairman for ten years of the Scottish Business School, which comprises the business studies departments of the Universities of Glasgow, Strathclyde, Edinburgh, Heriot Watt and Stirling. He is president of three technical societies and is deeply involved in inner-city problems. He is a founder member of the Prison Reform Trust.

> When they're young most people look naturally to their own selfish ambitions. If they're married, they look to improve their lot and that of their family. But after you reach a certain stage in life – I'd put it somewhere between forty-five and fifty-five – you suddenly feel you are as secure as you can be and you really ought to give something back to society. There's an old Jewish phrase which I think is worth repeating. It says: 'If I am not for myself, who will be for me?' That's the voice of selfishness and ambition and personal interest. It's the voice of the entrepreneur incidentally. But then the saying adds: 'If I am only for myself, what am I?' I think that's the voice of conscience and the voice of charity and the voice of doing something for the general good. It's a very interesting phrase and was thought up four thousand years ago.

Finniston maintains there is inescapable evidence that the corporate world has become more selfish and self-seeking.

> I think people go out to make a fast buck without worrying about the consequences. Who is affected is not their concern. The concern for the people for whom you are responsible by being given a position of influence and power and authority has gone. The Golden Handshake, the Golden Hello and Big Bang and the whizz kids have changed all that.

Finniston believes that the enterprise culture that has been fostered by the present government has to some extent fuelled a disregard for social responsibility.

> Encouraging enterprise is a good thing in many respects, but enterprise has been defined in people's minds as looking

> after your self-interest. How can you be satisfied with the economic state of a country when there are three million unemployed? Never mind if there are a few who don't want to work. People keep telling me hundreds and thousands of them don't want to work, but I never meet any of them. By definition, if there are hundreds and thousands of them, I must meet one or two of them as I go around, but I never do.

Morality, Sir Monty points out, is an integral part of a society's culture at any given time in its history, and in his view our moral conditions have changed radically. 'People don't feel ashamed these days even when they have been caught out,' he suggests in a tone of disbelief.

> The people who set the standards are no longer the older generation, the people who have lived their lives and come to some judgement on what life is all about. It's now the younger people, the people who make fortunes, like Richard Branson of Virgin, or even tennis stars, who set the standards. Extraordinary!

On the other hand, Finniston feels that the younger generation is having a favourable impact on the need to rid Britain of the 'them and us' syndrome that has plagued industry for so long and been at the root of so many of its ills.

> The next generation which is taking over the reins of industry is a generation who were not brought up in the same milieu that I was brought up in. I think they are becoming more conscious that the world is not right. They are arguing that it is not fair to have the 'haves' and the 'have-nots'; it's not fair to have a north and south divide. It takes time for this to develop and for people to recognise that they are partly responsible.

Finniston takes issue, however, with the view that the next generation of managers will find themselves working within a post-industrial society, where manufacturing industry has largely given way to a dependence on the service industries. He dismisses the whole concept of the post-industrial society as 'an economists' gimmick'.

> Economists in particular don't distinguish between the creation of wealth, which nowadays can be provided in large measure by machines, and the creation of employment, which in large measure requires other policies. We are a country of very poor natural resources and our standard of living depends upon high imports – it shouldn't but it does. These imports have to be paid for and what is interesting – and why manufacturing is vital to us – is that over the past hundred years, if not longer, seventy per cent of these imports have been paid for by the export of British manufactured goods. That's the important thing.

Finniston is convinced that too much emphasis is being placed on earnings from so-called 'invisible' exports. They, too, are subject to great competition, he argues. 'The Japanese are coming in through "Big Bang". We're small. If you take the largest ten banks in the world, there's not a single British bank among them. The first bank that comes into the ratings is NatWest or Barclays at number fifteen.'

Finniston's thesis is that the creation of wealth should come before the creation of employment,

> because it is the creation of wealth that creates employment, not in the thing that is creating the wealth but in other things. You recirculate it through taxation and through individual wealth. You can't afford the service industries unless you've got a good manufacturing base. I'm only talking about this country. If you lived in America or some of these other places where there's natural wealth under foot, like Saudi Arabia, that's a different matter. But the only appreciating resource that we've got is the talents and skills of the people to design, to manufacture, to produce and provide a service.

Finniston's own skills have certainly made an enormous contribution to the industrial growth of Britain. He seems to have sought very little in return, apart from the satisfaction of knowing, in his own words, that he has 'benefitted society'. He has very few of the traditional trappings of the successful captain of industry. 'I live a good life. I've been happily married to the same woman for fifty-odd years. I've got a nice apartment. I've never owned a house. I've always owned apartments because I was born in a tenement in Glasgow and I like flat-life.'

If he has one regret it is that government never saw fit to offer him another major job as challenging as his chairmanship of British Steel when he gave it up in 1976. He confides that he would have liked to have 'taken a crack at another big public objective'.

He was requested by Prime Minister James Callaghan to head a commission that looked into the future of the engineering profession in Britain, which kept him occupied for two and a half years. The resulting report, *Engineering our Future* brought about a minor revolution in the profession.

But Finniston still harbours the belief that the wealth of experience he acquired during his ten years at British Steel could have been put to better service for the nation. He is now, however, imparting that experience to the managers of tomorrow by his active involvement in a whole range of educational pursuits. Even in his mid-seventies, Finniston is showing no sign of flagging in his boundless energy or in the missionary zeal with which he preaches the gospel that a healthy industrial economy is in the best interests of society as a whole.

Sir Robert Haslam

Born: Bolton, Lancashire, 1923.
Educated: Bolton School; Birmingham University.

Sir Robert Haslam was appointed chairman of British Coal (formerly the National Coal Board) in September 1986. He had been deputy chairman and chairman-designate since November 1985. He is a former chairman of the British Steel Corporation and of Tate & Lyle plc.

A graduate of Birmingham University, where he took a BSc in coal-mining, he joined Manchester Collieries Ltd, in 1944. He qualified for his colliery manager's certificate in 1947 and is one of the longest-serving members of the Institute of Mining Engineers. In January 1947, the colliery company became part of the North Western Division of the newly formed National Coal Board.

Later in 1947 he joined the Nobel Division of Imperial Chemical Industries as a mining engineer specialising in explosives for the mining, quarrying and oil-prospecting industries. For the next ten years he travelled the world, visiting and working in mines and quarries in every continent. Subsequently, he had wide general management experience in three ICI divisions, becoming chairman of ICI Fibres, a main board director, personnel director and deputy chairman.

He is also a director of the Bank of England, a governor of the National Institute of Economic & Social Research, a governor of Henley Management College, chairman of Manchester Business School and an advisory director of Unilever. He is a former chairman of the Nationalised Industries Chairmen's Group. He has also been a non-executive chairman of Cable & Wireless, chairman of the North American Advisory Group, chairman of the Man-made Fibre Producers Committee and chairman of the European Synthetic Fibre Manufacturers.

SIR ROBERT HASLAM

He was made a freeman of the City of London in March 1985.

There have been a number of significant turning points in the career of Sir Robert Haslam, which he describes as 'negative accidents', but which turned out to have very positive results. It was, for example, a sheer fluke that he began his career as a mining engineer with Manchester Collieries Ltd. He had aimed to go to Cambridge to read geography, but failed the Latin entrance examination it was necessary to take in those days. In the event, he was accepted at Birmingham University, but just before he arrived he was informed that the geography department had been closed down because of austerity measures brought in during World War II. He therefore decided to read geology instead, but shortly afterwards he received notification that this department was also to be closed.

The next best option was to take a BSc degree in coal-mining – and that was how he ended up becoming a mining engineer instead of a teacher, which in all probability is the career he would have followed if he had managed to fulfil his original goal of studying geography.

Forty years later, after an enormously varied industrial career that has seen Haslam running a diverse range of businesses and involved in a wide variety of functions, from selling to personnel, events have turned full circle. His early days underground working alongside miners on the coal-face have imbued him with a special rapport with the thousands of miners he now oversees as chairman of British Coal.

> I worked in the coal mines for three years to obtain my colliery manager's certificate. As part of the training programme, you had to spend this period underground, of which eighteen months had to be spent on the coal face and during that time you did lots of jobs that mineworkers did. At times it seemed a bit strange to have a university degree and be working so physically hard but in many ways those three years were a very good period.

In particular, Haslam found the camaraderie he experienced working alongside mineworkers extremely rewarding.

> It was rather like being in the army on active service. The human relationships are very intense and therefore the learning curve is accelerated. I learned a great deal during that formative period about what made people tick and one saw what life was really like. Even though as a graduate I was something of an oddity, I was absorbed into the background after a time and people treated me as one of them. They behaved towards me as they would to anyone else and I found it a very valuable exposure.

Above all, it taught Haslam the 'common touch'. As he recalls: 'You had to be able to tangle with fairly tough and earthy, but likeable and well-meaning, people.' He stayed in digs in a colliery village at the time and found it equally possible to integrate easily into the local community. He detected no atmosphere of 'them and us', though he suspects that in similar circumstances today it might be a different story.

He had been promised that once he had obtained his colliery manager's certificate, he would be made an assistant manager. He received his certificate in July 1947 but the British coal industry had been nationalised in January of that year and his new bosses told him that in the changed circumstances they would not be able to carry out the undertaking he had been given. The disappointment Haslam inevitably felt at being let down in this way led to a second turning point in his career and one of those 'negative accidents' that ultimately proved to have a positive outcome.

He went to a local pub in the mining village where he was staying to drown his sorrows and found himself sitting next to a stranger who remarked on his dejected demeanour. It turned out that the stranger worked for ICI and he told Haslam that Britain's major chemical company was looking for mining engineers. Three days later Haslam was being interviewed for a job at ICI and he was offered the chance to become a technical services engineer in the Nobel Division, an offer he snapped up immediately.

The job involved visiting mining camps, quarries and oilfields all over the world selling explosives and it gave Haslam his first taste of the excitement of travel, something that has remained with him all his life.

> It wasn't really a management job. You operated very much as a self-contained individual. There were very few major countries I didn't visit during that time and travel was nothing like as easy as it is now. Going to South America, it would take you at least thirty-six hours to get to Lima, for example, in some clapped-out old aircraft. We had trips in those days that took as long as three months which not many people would undertake now. It was not all fun and games. I used to spend a lot of time in demanding places like the Andes and in remote parts of Africa.

He was eventually put in charge of the twenty people comprising the explosives technical services department and got his first taste of real management. After four years in the explosives division, his management potential had been spotted and moves were made to launch him on a management development programme of rotation to broaden his experience. He was offered a job on the production side, which would have entailed being a works superintendent. Not realising the long-term strategy behind the offer, Haslam turned it down, regarding it as an inferior job for someone with his mining engineering skills. He suspects that a black mark went firmly down against his name for turning down the job and when he was later asked to become personnel manager for that division of ICI he was left in no doubt that it was an offer he should not refuse.

> I was told that there wasn't going to be any nonsense like last time. I was going to be moved whether I liked it or not. In those days you could be a glorious amateur. You didn't have to be highly professional and experienced like a personnel manager has to be today. Everything was much freer. You could use commonsense much more. You weren't so bound by rules, legislation, case law or anything like that.

Although Haslam's lack of experience was no real handicap at a time when inspired amateurism prevailed, he did not face an easy task. During the years of World War II and for some time afterwards there had been a heavy demand for commercial and military explosives but by 1960 when Haslam was made personnel director of the Nobel Division of ICI the demand, particularly for military explosives, had dropped dramatically. It led to a period of sharp retrenchment and redundancies, a situation that at the time was very foreign to ICI which had been accustomed to unrestricted expansion in practically everything it undertook.

Having never had to face a situation of wholesale redundancies in the past, ICI's policies for dealing with them were out of date and inadequate.

> I was about thirty-four when I was made personnel director of the Nobel Division. I was only in that post for two years, but during that period we closed a lot of works. In the process we helped to reshape the whole of ICI's redundancy policy and the terms under which people left the company. Although the terms have continued to be remoulded and made more sophisticated, they basically emanate from that period. It was a very difficult period, because whereas retrenchment and redundancy are now something employees understand and accept, this was the first time it had ever happened in ICI since the war. People couldn't believe it. It was essentially confined to our division. We were a pioneer of a necessary but very undesirable kind of activity.

Haslam learned the hard way how to handle such a traumatic situation and how to some extent to play God when it became necessary to select the people who had to go.

> There are basically two kinds of redundancies. One is where you shut a works and everybody's in the same boat. That is an easier situation to handle. We always tried in ICI to offer people jobs elsewhere in the company whenever we could. The more difficult situation is where you have to apply some measure of selectivity. The question of people's status and their standing in the community can thereby be undermined.

The lesson Haslam learned from his ICI experience was that wherever possible redundancy should be on a voluntary basis if the trauma were to be kept to a minimum.

> So long as people can walk out of a room and say they have decided to leave on their terms, they retain their dignity. People argue that by adopting a voluntary approach you lose the good and the bad. It's primarily a matter of how you do the counselling as to who you lose. I'm not saying you may not lose a few good people but on balance it's worth that sacrifice rather than pursue an enforced redundancy policy.

Having to make hard decisions involving people is the only thing that gives Haslam sleepless nights.

> I don't worry about business in the money sense. I do worry about having to retire or remove somebody, particularly somebody close to me. I think that's the most difficult aspect of management. But you should never take the easy option. So often in my life, where I've made a mistake, it has been by taking the soft option. If you rationalise it by saying I don't want a row because I've got so much on my plate, it usually bounces back at you, often in an amplified form. If you cut corners just for a quiet life, you'll have trouble. It just builds up.

The next phase of Haslam's career was a totally different experience. He was plunged into the commercial side of the business, first as deputy regional sales manager for ICI's Southern Region and later – in 1963 – as commercial director of the Plastics Division. In those days sales of all ICI products were regionalised, a system he felt had shortcomings. He was a member of a working party which caused ICI to switch to a new approach under which each division took direct control of its own sales. It was as a result of this new approach that Haslam found himself in the Plastics Division, a more glamorous part of ICI, in contrast to the Nobel Division he had recently left. At about that time, plastics was one of two ICI divisions that had been selected to come under the scrutiny of McKinsey, the famous management consulting group. The consultants recommended that the Plastics Division be broken up into four groups, each with its own director. As a result, Haslam inherited what was then the plastic-film group, which was at an embryonic stage of development. But the business was growing very rapidly and expanding abroad. Haslam soon found himself in a position of having to make entrepreneurial decisions of staggering proportions.

> In those days, ICI had a sabbatical system and the chairman of my division went away for nearly four months. At this stage we were selling about three thousand tons of polyester film a year and my two closest lieutenants, my planning and marketing colleagues, persuaded me we should double the size of the plant at Dumfries in Scotland and that we should build another plant in Europe. We put these two expansion proposals through the ICI board while the divisional chairman was away. When he returned, he sent for me and said I must be stark crazy. He pointed out that we were then selling three thousand tons of the product and had sanctioned plans to build plants for twelve thousand tons.
>
> Well, I went off on holiday to Switzerland and on the way back I suddenly thought: Oh my God, what have I done? I went up to Scotland where by now they had dug the hole for this second plant and it looked absolutely enormous. I began to get cold feet, but these other two guys were totally positive and they were absolutely right. Those two plants came on stream at a time when we needed all the capacity they could provide. It was a period of risk-taking and setting horizons for growth rates which were different to anything I had experienced before.

By now Haslam was firmly on the management ladder at ICI and his broad experience of a wide variety of jobs and functions under the company's rotation scheme was clearly paying dividends.

> People often feel a sense of frustration that they are not moving up quickly enough when they join ICI. You have to go through a sort of incubation period while people weigh you up. You are not conscious of them weighing you up, but they do. The chances are that during the first eight or nine years you may appear to be treading water in the process of proving yourself. You can have the finest degree in the world, but at the end of the day you are judged as an

> individual and on your performance and then things begin to happen. Some people in ICI still come up by one functional channel and reach the top, but most emerging people get the management development treatment rather like I did.

Running the film group for ICI gave Haslam particular pleasure because it was the first time he had ever been fully in charge of a business, which he found very challenging. When he was promoted to deputy chairman of the Plastics Division in 1966 he remained in charge of the film group. But plastics as a whole had started to hit bad times. Sales of polythene and PVC, which had been two of ICI's mainstay products, had suddenly plummeted. It was a similar story when Haslam moved to become deputy chairman of ICI Fibres in 1969 with the intention that he would soon take over as chairman. Fibres had been one of ICI's big money spinners, but by the time Haslam joined the division nylon was already making a loss and polyester was about to collapse, having been a 'jewel in the crown'. As the patents had run out on many ICI fibre products, so competitors had jumped on the bandwagon and started building plants at a frenzied pace. The inevitable result was over-capacity in the market place followed by a vicious price war.

It was a foregone conclusion that Haslam would for the second time in his career find himself 'pitch-forked' into a retrenchment programme. This time it was on a much larger scale. The fibres division was an international business with plants in West Germany, Canada, the US, South Africa and Australia. When he took over ICI Fibres it employed around twenty-seven thousand people in Europe. He eventually whittled it down to eighteen thousand and his successors have since reduced the number even more dramatically. The impact of such a major reversal has left an indelible mark on Haslam's memory.

> In two years we went from a £32m profit, which I suppose in current rates would be in the region of £150m, to a £14m loss. So in two years flat, after riding on the crest of a wave, people who had been cock of the walk in ICI suddenly found themselves at the bottom of the league.

This was a time when Haslam learned the subtle art of keeping up appearances despite the fact that the world seemed to be collapsing all around him.

> The most important thing was just physically keeping up the morale. I had almost consciously to go out of the house in the morning with a smile fixed on my face, keep it on and breathe an air of absolute confidence when I was feeling anything but that way inclined. It was vital to give the impression at any rate that I and my board colleagues were in control of affairs and that we had a clear strategy that somehow was going to restore our business to its former glory.

Haslam believes this experience taught him the need to recognise that many products follow a predictable life cycle.

> First you have a unique product which has a highly profitable phase, but this frequently comes to an abrupt stop. Patent protection falls away and competitors can't wait to get in. Everybody thinks they can grab five per cent of everybody else's market without actually losing any of their own. So everyone expands rapidly and these collective misjudgements create a disaster situation. It doesn't matter who's running the show. Anybody who pretends they can buck these trends is under an illusion. You can only affect them peripherally. The momentum is there and it's like trying to change the course of a battleship. The important thing is to recognise that it is happening and take the relevant action.
>
> It can take up to ten years to readjust to this new market situation. By then the product will have reverted to being a reasonable business again – but not in a glamorous way as in the first phase. It becomes a 'cash cow' business in that you generate a lot of money from existing assets, with minimum investment.

The repercussions of such a turbulent period are not all disadvantageous, however. Haslam recalls a time when Sir Peter Allen, then the ICI main board director responsible for plastics, predicted at a small dinner party at the ICI guest house at Welwyn Garden City that the market price for polythene would drop from the current 4s a pound to 1s 6d a pound within six months. Everyone laughed it off as a typical piece of board-room exaggeration. But Allen was only wrong in that the price collapsed suddenly to 1s a pound. This, however, had the effect of dramatically expanding the market for polythene. It immediately became economical to use polythene for all kinds of products, like plastic bags, which nobody had ever contemplated previously. A host of new opportunities were opened up, once again revitalising the market.

Haslam points out that such experiences demand a great deal of positive thinking.

> It's a period of facing up to radically new cost levels. That means you've not only got to economise in manpower; you've got to bring new technology to bear on the problem. Inevitably, too, you will need to build more economical large-scale production units to meet the great new opportunities which have opened up.

Another danger Haslam warns about is the complacency that comes from being a successful innovator. 'ICI has been the first in the field with major products, such as polyester fibre and polythene. My impression is that if you invent something, you tend to have a built-in arrogance. You have a sort of halo around your head.'

But Haslam points out that the competitor who takes up the new technology when the patents expire does not suffer from this halo effect. Its only aim is to knock the market leader off the pedestal.

> The Japanese, of course, are past-masters at this. The more you make the running in this critical phase, the more you need to become sensitive to future technological and quality advances, because if you don't the other guy is going to leap-frog you. You can never rest on your laurels.

After having been in the thick of the battle for a number of years, Haslam found the transition to main board director in 1974 somewhat difficult to adjust to. After running a substantial international fibres business, it came as something of a cultural shock to find himself sitting in ICI's headquarters with only a secretary to command. He became the product director on the board for both paints and fibres and also territorial director for India and Pakistan, but he had to work in each case through the chief executive who was charged with running the business.

Haslam found this a rather passive role compared to running a business himself, so when he was asked to become ICI's personnel director he jumped at the opportunity to tackle a job which appeared to have a higher executive content. It meant, too, that he would have some troops of his own again. By this time the personnel function in ICI had ceased to be the domain of inspired amateurs. Haslam was backed up by a four-man team of senior colleagues, all of whom were highly professional. One was responsible for industrial relations and union negotiations. Another looked after the monthly staff employees. A third was entirely concerned with management development and career planning and the fourth acted as a one-man think-tank, whose task was to advise on how ICI's personnel policies should evolve in future.

It did not bother Haslam that he had to rely to a large degree on the expertise of others to perform his own job well.

> I think the art of moving around as I have done in my career into different products and functions and into various industries is the ability to sum up quickly your close colleagues. You can never hope to achieve the professionalism of those who have been in a single business all their lives and hence you need quickly to get to know those whose opinions you can trust. These may not always be the people who sparkle a great deal because they often have a maverick quality. If you are to move about in the senior echelons of industry, this is an important ability to develop.
>
> Some people are incredibly reactive. They get into discussion with a neighbour on Concorde going to New York and when they get back they say they've got the finest idea since sliced bread. Such colleagues tend to be great achievers, but you have to restrain their worst excesses. I've seen quite brilliant people in ICI who throw off sparkling ideas like an emery wheel, but only one in ten of their ideas is likely to

> be viable. On the other hand, other people display a great sense of diffidence but often have admirable ideas which they are reluctant to reveal. Such people need drawing out.

Haslam paints the picture of a corporate impresario who recognises the various talents and skills of those around him and orchestrates events so that these talents may be used to the greatest benefit of the enterprise. But he pinpoints another factor that influences the way the players perform together – company culture.

> People talk about the role of chairman or chief executive as though these are clear definitive roles. These can be very variable depending on the culture of the company. For example, ICI doesn't have a chief executive and operates on a consensus basis with the chairman acting as a *primus inter pares*. We rarely took a vote sitting around the board table. If there was a strong majority in favour of a particular action, we would go to great lengths to persuade the minority of the error of their ways.

Many other companies have a more autocratic culture in that the chairman and chief executive will have a disproportionate say in what happens. 'The other board members will expect to have their say, but at the end of the day they expect, and accept, that the chairman should decide.'

The next phase of Haslam's career was one where he moved about from company to company rather than from function to function. While serving as deputy chairman of ICI he became ill and was advised to take life a little more quietly. He therefore took on the chairmanship of Tate & Lyle on a part-time basis. That was as much as he felt he could cope with for a while, but he was soon to be 'prevailed upon by government' to become chairman of British Steel in double harness with the Tate & Lyle job.

> I thought at the time it was a crazy thing to agree to and early events seemed to confirm this. In the end, it worked out very much better than expected, essentially because the two companies had outstanding chief executives, both of

> whom eventually succeeded me as chairman. But it was still very difficult, because every day I was in London I was moving from one business to the other and they could not have been more different in character. It was a particularly testing time at British Steel as we were still engaged in the major retrenchment exercise and we also had the very difficult task of keeping the steel mills operating during the miners' strike.

It was during this time, moving from one company to another, that Haslam learned the true meaning of what it is to be an adaptable manager. These companies all had able and high-calibre people who knew their respective businesses very well, but his objective was to inject his own ideas into the decision-making process in the hope that this would produce an added beneficial dimension. 'Many companies, however successful, tend to be somewhat inbred and for this reason people often welcome an injection of new thinking into their affairs.'

Whereas Haslam has found that a detached outside perspective has proved to be valuable in several of the companies he has served as a board member, his early intimate knowledge of the coal industry was equally beneficial when he was asked to become chairman of British Coal, bringing his career full circle.

> It's amazing, even after a forty-year gap, that I feel I still have a rapport with most mineworkers because of my early days in the industry. I can also listen to a conversation between mining engineers and understand ninety-five per cent of it, even after all these years. They've got a particular jargon. Very occasionally a new phrase disconcertingly emerges which I have never heard before.

Haslam's exposure to the worldwide business scene nevertheless gives him an extra dimension with which to tackle the British Coal job. The combination of a broad industrial experience and a close understanding of how the typical mineworker views life gave him the confidence to take on a responsibility which a less courageous man might well have ducked.

> In a way this job at British Coal is a particularly gruelling

> one. The other side of the coin is that it is very satisfying and rewarding because it stretches me in every possible way. You've really got to be able to play all the keys on the piano on this one. It's enjoyable but inevitably has some masochistic undertones!

Haslam admits that being the focal point of all the national publicity that inevitably surrounds the British coal industry is not something that he relishes.

> I don't find that easy and never will. I find TV particularly demanding, but it's almost impossible to avoid it. I feel reasonably relaxed if I am interviewed on my own ground, but find TV stations rather stressful and alien situations.
>
> With somebody like Mr Scargill, I think you've got to make yourself as available to the media as you can. I think most people felt that during the early stages of the miners' strike the British Coal balance with Scargill was not strong enough. It's not a thing I'm particularly good at, but I do try to put over our viewpoint.

As far as the perks of the job are concerned, Haslam looks back at his ICI days with a certain amount of nostalgia. He travelled widely in those days, often accompanied by his wife, and they lived for two years in the United States where he was responsible for ICI's affairs in North and South America. Life as the head of British Coal is a lot less glamorous.

> Going to Blackpool or Scarborough is now an adventure. I get jet-lag flying to Manchester! My wife and I feel somewhat denied. Obviously I can go to the US or China to see mining practices there if I choose to, but it's not easy to get away. I feel more tied down than I've ever been before.

Haslam also feels deprived of some of the cultural facilities that were available to him during his ICI days for entertaining customers and associates. Like most major private-sector companies ICI has facilities reserved for it at many of the events that dominate the social calendar, such as Glyndebourne, Ascot and Wimbledon. There are no such privileges for the senior executives of a nationalised industry like British Coal. 'I am dependent on people with whom I have been associated in the past inviting me and I must say they could not have been more gracious.'

Despite such curbs on his social life, Haslam rarely spends an evening at home during the week. He is in such demand as a speaker that he has had to make a rule that he will no longer accept invitations to functions that are unconnected with the coal industry.

> The biggest problem is containing the number of speeches you have to give, because despite the fact the industry has contracted, all the institutions that relate to our industry are still flourishing. A lot of people retire from industry and spend a great deal of effort on these activities. So the demands on your time to speak at a wide range of institution meetings and dinner functions are legion.

Although Haslam has been obliged to cut back on business travel, he and his wife still do a fair amount of travel for personal pleasure and grab as many long weekends as they can to get away from it all, making flying visits to the Mediterranean. They have both been occasional golfers, which they still enjoy when on holiday in Spain or Portugal. But although they live on the edge of Wentworth Golf Course, Lady Haslam prefers gardening when at home.

Looking back on his varied career, Haslam is somewhat guarded about passing on any pet theories on how to manage at the top. If his successor at British Coal were appointed from within the corporation he considers that it would be impertinent to tell him how the job should be done. He does, however, have some general advice for anyone coming into British Coal from the outside.

> In this industry you've got to be very much an 'open-door' person. You've got to be prepared to listen to a lot of varied opinions about many difficult problems, assess the people who give you those opinions and at the end of the day you've got to be very decisive and determined. If I analyse the bosses I've worked for, the ones who irritated

me the most were the ones who were indecisive and who constantly asked for more information just to delay making a decision.

When you are appointed a chairman of a nationalised industry, you are given clear objectives by your Secretary of State, and you have to see that your immediate colleagues and indeed the whole team are aware of, and are striving to achieve, these objectives. In both British Coal and British Steel I have been enormously impressed by the ability and dedication of my colleagues, particularly when one recognises the totally inadequate rewards they receive in comparison with their opposite numbers in the private sector. Sadly, despite recently introduced performance bonus schemes, this gap is still widening.

It is important to create, as I've tried to do at British Coal, a sense of challenge. If I look back on the people who have led me very well in the past, it was those who were able to create and sustain just such a sense of challenge. When I was in the Nobel Division of ICI, the chairman was one of the most diminutive of men. He was about five-feet tall, but he had an enormous ability to make you feel that you had been given a real challenge and it seemed all-important to discharge it to his satisfaction and he was equally praising of your achievement. This is true leadership.

You've got to be very conscious too of people's personal problems and relationships. It is particularly important, whatever their preoccupations, that managers find time to discuss and help with such problems. In terms of the business they probably don't matter a great deal, but it's very important if you're going to develop the right team spirit.

Sir Hector Laing

Born: Edinburgh, 1923.
Educated: Loretto School, Scotland; Jesus College, Cambridge.

Sir Hector Laing is chairman of United Biscuits (Holdings) plc, a company capitalised at £1.4 bn that employs thirty thousand people and produces five billion food packets every year – the equivalent to one for every person on earth. He was knighted in the 1978 New Year's Honours List.

He joined the family firm of McVitie & Price in 1947 and became chairman in 1963. He was appointed managing director of United Biscuits in 1964 and took over as chairman in 1972.

He is a director of the Bank of England and of Exxon Corporation Inc. He is chairman of Business in the Community both in Scotland and England, and is joint-chairman of the Per Cent Club, a group of companies that pledge a proportion of their income to the community. He is governor of the National Institute of Economic and Social Research and a member of the Council for Industry & Higher Education.

From 1977 to 1979 he was chairman of the Food & Drink Industries Council.

He is joint-treasurer of the Conservative Party.

There was never a time in Sir Hector Laing's life when it ever occurred to him to work for any other company than the family business, originally called McVitie & Price and now known as United Biscuits. He was steeped in the business from an early age. When only five years old, he used to go into the bakery with his father before school just for fun. He and his brother would take delight in cutting out oat cakes. At school he did 'extraordinarily badly' by his own admission and he also failed to obtain a degree in agriculture at Cambridge University, but with his sights firmly fixed on a career in the family business, such academic shortcomings represented no real handicap.

He served with the 3rd Battalion of the Scots Guards during the war, but finally, in 1947, he was able to fulfil his long-cherished ambition to savour company life.

> From the very first day I enjoyed it. There was no doubt in my mind what I would do and I've never regretted going into the business because we've seen it grow enormously. When I joined the company it was capitalised at about £4m and it is now capitalised at about £1.4bn. That has all been great fun.

Laing could have added that it is also now a company that employs tens of thousands of people and produces a phenomenal amount of food snacks. It is best known for its mouth-watering digestive biscuits, but some staggering statistics graphically illustrate the incredible production rate at United Biscuits. It produces five billion food packets every year; that's one for every single person on earth. Each week the company produces biscuits equivalent in weight to 1,200 elephants. If the group's total annual output in biscuits were laid edge to edge, they would stretch twice to the moon and back, or forty-eight times around the equator. The United Biscuit's chairman could never have guessed in his early days with the firm that it would grow into such a huge food manufacturer. Then, it only commanded a small proportion of the UK biscuit market.

He started by doing stints in the three main factories in London, Manchester and Edinburgh, often working very long hours. For a period, he worked in the Manchester factory from 3am until 5pm, going to bed at 7pm so he could get up in time for the next day's duty. He regards this somewhat gruelling routine as having been a vital part of his training.

> Part of the advice one would want to give to any young person today is to thoroughly know your business by working on the factory floor. I came to understand fully about making biscuits and if you make things right you

have a chance of selling them – as the Japanese have amply demonstrated. If you fail to make them right, then all the marketing and computers in the world won't help you.

Laing is convinced that businesses which are run by people who have little understanding of the products being made are ultimately doomed to failure.

I think the shoemaker should stick to his last. Most of the conglomerates which were made up of a disparate collection of businesses have failed. The best businesses over a long period of time have been the ones with a single thrust. Ours happens to be food. It's a wider range of food than when we started, which was only in biscuits. If you can sell biscuits, you can probably sell crisps, but it doesn't mean to say that if you can sell these you can sell dresses or bicycles.

Although Laing started at the bottom of the ladder, he admits that the fact he and his brother inherited control of the business early on in their careers helped them to climb the hierarchy rather swiftly. He took over the firm with some very clear ambitions. In those days it was common for industrialists to go to the United States to learn how major companies should best be run. The Americans were setting the pace. Laing wanted to make such a good job of the London factory that the reverse would be the case – that the Americans would want to cross the Atlantic to inspect the exemplary way the British ran things.

Secondly, I wanted to create a factory where nobody would ever have to do any physical work. We achieved both goals. From 1953 to 1964 we built up that factory into perhaps the second largest of its kind in the world and certainly the largest and best in Europe.

Laing's desire to reduce physical exertion stemmed from personal experience during his early days on the shop floor. 'When I started I was carrying flour sacks on my back, digging fat out of boxes, syrup out of barrels, that sort of thing. We were the first to automate all that.' He acknowledges, however, that striving for automation brings other problems in its wake.

> It tends to make life a bit dull at work and we've tried to come to terms with that. It also has implications in terms of the number of jobs, in that you need far fewer people. When I started it was about two hundred people per ton and now we produce five tons an hour with three people. So it displaces people. On the other hand, if you're making something the world wants, by making it as the lowest cost supplier, you can usually expand your work-force. But even if you can't you have to be the lowest cost supplier if you possibly can. When you are, you've got a good business.

A number of key people influenced Laing during his early impressionable years in the company. One was his grandfather, whom he describes as,

> a compassionate employer – compassionate by those days' standards, not by today's standards. So one set out with a policy of having good human relations and my friendship with Marcus Sieff (now president of Marks & Spencer) dating back to 1953 has also had an influence. I think we both recognised early on – perhaps he before me – the importance of good human relations and our policies have, I believe, been beneficial to both our businesses.

Another mentor Laing remembers with affection was George Miller, who was the sales manager at the London factory, who taught him how important it was to have 'a main thrust' in a business.

> In our case that was to make a very short list of high-quality biscuits. Before the war, that factory had made 384 different biscuits. We cut it to four and those four are still our major selling products and the foundation of our business. I learned a lot from him and his ability to see what had gone wrong from a sales point of view.

Someone who possibly had more influence on Laing than anyone else was the late Sir Douglas Crawford, formerly chairman of Wm Crawford & Sons, which became part of United Biscuits in 1962 when Sir Douglas became vice-chairman until his retirement in 1974. Laing thought very highly of Sir Douglas, whom he saw as 'a man of great integrity and absolutely straightforward'. Crawford taught Laing 'the value of low cunning and lovable dimness!'

Laing has striven hard over the years to implement the enlightened human relations policies he first learned from his grandfather. He has, for example, adopted a single-status policy at United Biscuits, which, among other things, ensures that the same company pension scheme applies equally to top management and the rank and file.

> I think you have to look after people both at work and when they retire and we inflation-proofed our pension scheme during the whole of that pretty dreadful time when inflation was running at over twenty per cent. We try to see that conditions at work are such that if I, to make it personal, was working in a particular factory, I would find them as congenial as they could reasonably be. I think if one looks at life and says: 'If I was doing that job, what are the conditions I would like to work in?', and then put them into operation, people will probably think it's about right.

Laing has never felt that being a compassionate employer has been at odds with doing the right thing commercially. Even when it is necessary to close down factories it can be done with compassion, in his view. 'You've got to have a work-force that believes in you. Therefore, you've got to give it leadership and you've got to be seen. I think a business can hardly fail if it's got that sort of spirit. If the work-force is working against you, it can hardly win.'

These beliefs were put to the test when United Biscuits was obliged to close one of its main factories in Liverpool.

> It was a ghastly thing to have to do – in Liverpool of all places. We took four years to do it, partly so people would get accustomed to the idea, and it was fantastic that during those four years people worked at least as hard and as well as they had in the previous four. We tried every way to find them alternative jobs.

The pending closure fell foul of the Church, however, and Laing was confronted with a deputation of protesting bishops.

> They said what I was doing was terrible and in a way, from the people's point of view, it was. But we employ thirty thousand people and therefore one has to look after the majority, however hard it may be on a relatively few – one thousand people in that particular case. But it's not something one enjoys doing.

In Laing's opinion, a manager becomes increasingly sensitive to the needs of others as he gets older and more experienced.

> When one is young and brash – and I think I was brash – one is inclined to brush people aside because you know what you want and you are determined to get it, whereas when one has seen some of the problems of the world, I think one is probably more tolerant.

Motivating employees is another issue to which Laing has given much thought. 'Choose people well, train them well, give them their heads, but you have to monitor their performance as well,' he advises. 'I'm a great delegator, but it is important to delegate to those who are capable of carrying through the task and you must have a good report-back system.'

Communicating well to the troops is another important aspect of senior management, in Laing's opinion. He cites the example shown by Viscount Montgomery in World War II. Laing, who fought under the famous military leader, recalls that the troops always had great confidence in him because he was very visible.

> He told us what he was going to do and we knew some people were going to get killed, but that's just life. It's the same with closing a factory. Some are going to have to go. But if you see the top man around the business you are able to look him in the eye and tell whether you can trust him or not.

Laing has applied the Mongomery approach to business.

> We employ 30,000 people in the UK business and I speak

> to 15,000 of them every year in groups of 200 or less, because I think the Japanese have shown what good human relations can achieve. Too many managers in this country want to sit in their offices and write memos. If people can see that you know your job, that you work probably harder than they do, that you communicate with them and tell them what you're doing, they will respect you. They may not like you, but they will respect you and they will work well for you.

Laing has developed some rather unconventional methods for communicating to his troops. He used to go around with a jug of orange juice to drum home to people that it is impossible to earn more unless more is produced.

> I used to pour the orange juice, which represented the added value in our products, into four separate glasses. I poured 70 per cent of it into a glass representing the wages paid to those of us who work in the businesss, 20 per cent into a glass representing what was ploughed back by way of reinvestment in plant and machinery, 5 per cent into a glass representing dividends and 5 per cent into a glass representing tax.
>
> What I tried to teach people was that if we didn't increase the added value, but took more of it and put it in our pockets, the only place we could take it from was the glass marked reinvestment and that makes people unemployed quicker than anything – and permanently. I think perhaps on the whole people understand that better than they used to.

He maintains there are no short cuts to managing effectively. 'The work-force can pick out a fraud very easily or someone who's just glossing things over. It's much better to look people in the eye and tell them the truth.'

In Laing's view, getting to the top in management by climbing up through the ranks is fifty per cent luck, but when the opportunities present themselves, they have to be grasped, and that often requires courage. The person who never takes risks never achieves anything in his view. One of his favourite sayings is that:

> The man who never makes a mistake works for somebody who does. There's got to be an element of the entrepreneur. You've got to be ambitious, not necessarily for yourself, but for your company to be among the best in the world and you've got to strive to get it there. You've got to ensure that your products are really first class and you have to have first-class people at every level. Then you have a first-class business.

Laing has never had any problems about getting to grips with long-term strategy. It is not always possible to give adequate thought to the future when caught up in the day-to-day running of an operation, but if you live the business, as Sir Hector unashamedly does, there are always less hectic times to mull over major issues. He tends to ponder on such weighty matters in the bath or while gardening.

One of the issues that called for more profound thought than usual was the direction United Biscuits should take after its products had come to command the lion's share of the market and couldn't be expected to squeeze out many more sales.

> When I started we only had about five per cent of the biscuit trade. We now have close on fifty per cent. When you saw that happening you realised you had to go into other things.
>
> The other thing that is important is that I don't think you can get anything on the cheap. Therefore, if you really want to move the business forward and make it a great business, you've got to live it. I tell the young people joining us that the great division in their lives, if they climb in the business, is the division between the company and their family. If they're not very careful, the family will lose out every time and that causes a lot of problems in our society. I think you've got to be fair about how much time you give the family. I ask nobody to work seven days a week or twelve hours a day, except in very limited periods when we all have to.

Laing has often been accused of being a workaholic himself, but he denies it. He has an understanding with his wife that weekends are sacrosanct and the couple always enjoy six weeks' holiday together every year. 'That's not to say when you're gardening or on holiday that the wheels stop turning and you don't have any ideas.' Laing's favourite technique for resolving major business problems is to 'chew things over'. Unlike many top executives, he doesn't believe in committing thorny issues to paper. He prefers instead to hold meetings with his colleagues and to talk things through until a solution emerges.

> I will sometimes arrange to discuss things on three successive Mondays, for example, or three successive months perhaps, because you never have to take a quick decision in a business, and out of the talking with people who respond to your way of working the right answer very often comes – the decisions mostly take themselves.

One of the few occasions that United Biscuits ever took a hasty decision was when it bought a company in Spain at a time when it felt under pressure to expand into Europe. It was before Spain had joined the Common Market and United Biscuits' efforts to acquire a suitable company in one of the EEC countries had come to nought. Laing admits that the Spanish company was bought out of desperation and it cost United Biscuits dearly.

> We regretted the decision for the next ten years. It taught me the lesson that you should never do something because you feel you've got to. You should wait until the right opportunity comes along. You should look for the right company if you're intending to buy one, the right situation in the right country and then move quickly. But don't just jump in because you feel you've got to.

The top executive who is constantly looking ahead rather than backwards will rarely steer his company into a tight corner, in Laing's view. He suggests the top man should repeatedly be asking himself: 'What if . . .?' Because if you don't say 'What if?' you'll be saying: 'If only . . .'

Laing points out that this approach generates a lot of ideas, many of which will be worthless, as happens in a brainstorming session. But, he maintains, if you don't throw up a lot of worthless ideas you are unlikely to come up with sensible ones either.

Laing pauses to collect his thoughts when considering what was perhaps the most difficult decision of his long career. He eventually concludes that it involved another acquisition – this time the American firm of Keebler in 1974.

> We paid over $50m for it, and that, for a small British company in those days going into a market where British companies hadn't been notably successful, was seen as a very big commitment. Our shares plummeted because the City felt we had taken a great risk. But it turned out to be one of the most marvellous things we ever did. It has done so much for us. Not only has it made a very good profit, but getting a bit of the American ethos into the business has been a good thing as well.

He was, however, disappointed when in 1985 a planned merger with the Imperial Group failed to go ahead. The merger would have resulted in by far and away Britain's largest food company and placed it among the world league of major food groups, capitalised at around £5bn. But the grand design was torpedoed when Lord Hanson made a bid for Imperial that shareholders found impossible to resist. The government also intervened on the grounds that a small part of the proposed merger, relating to the crisp business, contravened the monopolies law.

> The idea behind trying to get together with Imperial was to create a world-size food company with, as it happened, tobacco money to back it up, because the cashflow from tobacco is much more than the tobacco business actually requires to sustain it. I was going to be chairman and chief executive and Bob Clarke, my chief executive, was going to run the food side. That seemed to me to be a nice balance – good for our shareholders, good for our company and good for the country, as I saw it.

Laing does not blame the shareholders for opting for the Hanson offer.

> But as far as Great Britain Ltd was concerned and building a food industry that would have a major part to play

> in China and Brazil and other developing countries, I was sorry the shareholders took the view that they did. What I do criticise is the City taking a short-term view. I find it galling that they seem to keep looking for jam today.
>
> We are not going to establish British companies across Europe, let alone across the world, if our monopolies legislation disallows mergers of major companies within one industry – the only way they are going to be strong enough to do it. The problem is compounded when we allow our leading businesses – Rowntree and perhaps Cadbury's and others – to be bought up by foreign predators so that our muscle is destroyed.

Anyone running a major company in Britain today needs to be keenly aware of the international scene in Laing's opinion.

> We are only fifty million people in this country and if you're going to run a decent-size business at all, you need to be looking at the horizon. This may sound harsh, but it seems to me that when we lost our empire our eyes came down from the horizon and looked at our feet. Since 1979 we have just begun to have confidence in ourselves to raise our eyes to the horizon again. If we had paid more attention to what the Japanese were doing we would perhaps not be so subject to their products as we are.

Laing broadens his horizons by travelling a lot and by taking part in a large number of outside activities. 'I think you should get to know as many people as you can the further up the business you are,' he says. He travels to the US at least once a month and enjoys getting out and about. 'I travel in comfort,' he adds to explain why he finds it less of a hassle than many businessmen. 'I travel first class and I take Concorde whenever I can. I think it's important to keep your eyes open. It's not enough to *say* that things can be done differently or better. You have to see them first hand. I suppose it's called "Management by Walking About".'

As a director of the Bank of England, Laing, who confesses that finance has never been his strong point, broadens his horizons on the economic front. While he could equally get the information from other sources, he finds that 'going there every week, you hear about what's going on, which is a great help.'

Laing has some strong convictions about the role major companies should play in the community as a whole. He is chairman of Business in the Community and of the Scottish BIC, an organisation that supports enterprise agencies and arranges the secondment of experienced senior executives to fledgling small firms. He believes that the financial support companies give to charitable works can, and should, be quantified. To do something concrete in this direction, Laing hit on the idea of forming what he wanted to call the One Per Cent Club, all the corporate members of which would pledge one per cent of their UK pre-tax income to the community. Unable to persuade other firms to commit to such a specific amount, he arrived at a compromise by forming the Per Cent Club, which has 120 corporate members giving not less than a half per cent of their annual UK pre-tax income to the community.

United Biscuits have pledged a one per cent contribution, which in 1988 amounted to £1m. Critics of the idea argue that companies can achieve the same purpose by paying out good dividends, but Laing questions whether much of this money finds its way back into the community.

> When I was a youngster much charitable giving came from wealthy families. As they became progressively more heavily taxed, that responsibility, instead of going to companies, went to government and government has been seen to do it very badly. So we are now getting it back into the corporate sector.

Laing feels strongly that the chief executive of a company should define, as he has done at United Biscuits, exactly what its responsibilities to the community are.

> He should make it known within the company that this is one of his priorities, that the whole board supports it and that a percentage of the profits should be devoted to it. Not only do we do that at United Biscuits, we also second one manager for every two thousand employees. So we've got

fifteen to sixteen managers seconded to various bodies in this country that need help.

Laing rejects the view held by some people that managers from major corporations are unsuitable for giving advice to small firms because they live in two different worlds.

If you take one of our accountants who might spend a day a month with a small business, the fact that the business is small and we're big doesn't matter at all. The governing factors, whether it be marketing or computers or finance, are the same for a big or small company. The scale of the problems will be different, but a chap who can run ICI, if he can be bothered to help a small business, will do it very well from his experience.

Laing accepts that to some extent he was born with a silver spoon in his mouth. 'I've never had a money worry,' he admits in all honesty,

and of course that's very lucky, but it's also a responsibility. It's what you do with the money that counts. In a lot of families, if you've plenty of money when you're young you question the necessity of work. My ethos was I've got a lot of money, but I've got to look after the people as far as I can who have helped to produce it and I am going to make it grow bigger for our successors. The oak tree has got to grow all the time.

'That probably sounds pompous,' adds Laing apologetically, reflecting on what he had just said. 'I love our business and I take great pride in it. I was lucky being a major shareholder. Of course my salary is important to me, but it doesn't give me my life style. That has come from the family.'

Inheriting wealth has not led Laing into a flamboyant lifestyle by any means. His two concessions to luxury appear to be a passion for fast cars – he is the proud owner of a turbo-Bentley – and a 5,000 acre estate in Scotland. Apart from that, his life is devoid of ostentation. 'What my wife and I really like doing are the very simple things, like gardening and walking,' he adds.

'We go abroad for a week or ten days every year, but I think we have a very simple life compared with many. We don't have luxury yachts or go to expensive hotels all the time.'

Laing also has very modest tastes in food. He favours the plain dishes when eating at home, such as a plate of mince, sardines, spaghetti or bacon and eggs. 'But every now and again it's jolly nice to go out and have an absolutely top-class meal in a super restaurant,' he adds with relish.

Laing acknowledges that the up-and-coming generation of managers are faced with a much faster-paced world than he has operated in most of his life, but he is not convinced it is any more difficult to be an executive today than in the past. He points to the fact that the Atlantic can now be crossed in three and a half hours as indisputable evidence that the pace has hotted up, but in his view, the next generation will assimilate such changes.

> It's interesting that if you have a machine wrapping biscuits at 50 a minute and it is increased to 70 a minute, the operators who have been doing it at 50 find it very difficult to adapt, but the new operators who come in at 70 cope with it easily. It's just like young people today dealing with computers. They are all growing up with the computer effortlessly.

The United Biscuits chairman is, however, concerned that today's executive finds himself working in a business environment that appears to be in danger of moral decline. He recently drew up an ethics policy for United Biscuits, which he expects all his managers to endorse, because 'as a business becomes bigger and bigger – we now have operations in Japan, America and Belgium as well as the UK – I think the family ethics drawn up by the founders can gradually get eroded or watered down.'

Another concern of Laing's is the shift from private to institutional shareholders.

> Fund managers are intent on doing their best for their funds and have no interest whatsoever in the businesses they invest in or the people who are producing the profits. I am not saying this is universal, of course, but I think the pressure from the City on industry to maximise profits tends to make them take short cuts. One reason I have written

> this code of ethics is that no one has to take short cuts ever. You have to keep the City informed about what's going on, but I think you can run a business – and I hope we do – to the highest moral standards whether it's today or in the 1900s.

Laing feels the problem is exacerbated by the tendency today for the corporate world to live in the short term. In the UK and the US a company's financial performance is judged at quarterly intervals. Laing believes that countries like Japan and West Germany which take a more long-term attitude to performance are less subjected to such pressures.

> I believe in a competitive world, but at the same time I think we have got to be laying sound foundations for future growth and if we are constantly pressured into satisfying stock-market expectations, which are short-term, or under threat of take-over, we will not be investing enough for the long-term development of our businesses.

Laing is convinced that the future generation of managers need have no fear of what lays in store from the so-called post-industrial society. He simply doesn't believe in it. 'I've heard it said that we are going to be a service economy. Well, we can't be a service economy because that doesn't actually make anything.' Rather, Laing believes the UK has got to reassert itself as a manufacturing economy.

> Make what the world wants and the world will come for it. Look at the mess British Steel got into. It's now one of the best steel companies in the world. The errors we made in the 1960s and 1970s can, and are, being corrected. OK, give it ten years and perhaps only 20 per cent will be producing what 60 per cent or 70 per cent were twenty-five years ago. We can go on producing more and more with less and less people. I can see the day when our London factory will be totally automatic.

This, Laing believes, will demand an entirely different approach to work with the emphasis on flexibility.

> I'm going to say something which the Church won't like – and I go to church every Sunday. Our plants have got to work seven days a week, but with people working a four-day week. Or you can forget the week as a unit of work altogether and you can say: 'I will contract you for a certain number of hours.' The company has then got to say: 'If you want to take three months' holiday, good luck to you provided the contracted hours are worked.' The plants have got to keep going, but I think we can make working hours much more flexible.

Laing would also like to see a fundamental reappraisal of the way unions operate. 'I would like to see the union structure changed totally,' he says uncompromisingly.

> We don't want *trades* unions, we want unions. The food industry should have one union, just like in Japan and West Germany – and then totally flexible hours. I think you could play so many tunes on it that not only would we be producing much more efficiently and economically, but people could have a better quality of life too.

Giving employees a greater say in how their companies operate could be an important step towards such a goal, but Laing is opposed to the appointment of worker directors, as is the practice in Scandinavia. 'I think everybody who joins a company in any capacity should, if he's got the capability, be able to reach board level. But I don't think you should just appoint somebody and say he's a worker director. I just don't believe in that.'

Laing firmly believes, however, in assisted share purchase and profit-sharing schemes, which give all employees the opportunity to share in a company's financial achievements. He also maintains that if the brain drain is to be halted there needs to be an upward hike in salaries in Britain. While he considers that salaries in the City have grown out of all proportion, he is convinced that corporate managers are falling behind in the remuneration they receive.

> If we want to keep the best scientists and the best engineers in this country, we'd better do two things: we'd better attract

them with good pay and we'd better train them right and give them the proper facilities. As we become richer as a country we shall be able to do all these things. We did get damn poor, you know.

Laing still has one outstanding ambition before he retires. Having seen United Biscuits 'gain a toehold in Brazil', he would like to see the company expand into China. He faces the prospect of retirement with the same level-headed commonsense approach with which he has tackled most of the issues that have confronted him in his long career.

I have been in the company forty years. I've been chief executive and/or chairman for twenty-five years and the tendency is to think you're indispensable and you have to stay on until you're seventy-five, as some people do.

I think one wants to go at a time when people still want you to stay, rather than stay until people want you to go. If you've been pretty dominant in a company I don't think you know when that time has actually arrived. So I shall go when people rather wished I stayed in a way. But it's your responsibility to see that your successors are properly groomed to take over.

But there's no question of Laing fading completely from the corporate scene.

I'm not going to sit back and watch TV. In retirement I hope my company will provide me with an office and a secretary, so that I can go on contributing to society from my experience. I would like to work on lots of things in the inner cities and the community.

Sir Austin Pearce

Born: Plymouth, Devon, 1921.
Educated: Devonport High School; Birmingham University.

Sir Austin Pearce is a former chairman of Esso Petroleum Co and British Aerospace. He was knighted in 1980.

He joined AGWI Petroleum Co, later to become Esso, in 1945 as a technical assistant at Fawley Refinery. He became managing director of Esso in 1968 and was chairman from 1972 to 1980. He was president of the Institute of Petroleum from 1968 to 1970 and president of the UK Petroleum Industries Association from 1979 to 1980.

In 1976 he became a member of the organising committee charged with the responsibility of welding a disparate group of UK aircraft companies into the nationalised British Aerospace group. Four years later, as chairman of BAe, he was asked by the government to prepare the group for privatisation. From 1982 to 1983, he was president of the Society of British Aerospace Companies.

He is vice-chairman of the Royal Bank of Scotland and was chairman of Williams & Glyn's Bank from 1983 to 1985.

He is chairman of Oxford Instruments Group and a non-executive director of Pearl Group, Jaguar and Smiths Industries.

He was a member of the President's Advisory Committee of the Confederation of British Industry from 1982 to 1988 and is currently a member of the Takeover Panel.

In addition, he is chairman of the trustees of the Science Museum and pro-chancellor of Surrey University.

Someone once asked Sir Austin Pearce when he first decided to become chairman of Esso. He answered that it was when the job was offered to him. His entire career in industry seems to have been a series of opportunities seized with relish. Not for him the carefully charted route to the top. 'If I'm given a challenge I have to have a go at it,' he admits, reflecting on the guiding principles that have taken him to the top of two major industries. 'I've had a number of opportunities and taking them, particularly in the oil industry, has sometimes been a desperate gamble.'

His eyes light up at the recollection of some of the challenges he has tackled that would have daunted the more faint-hearted. There was one classic occasion when the flare went out at Fawley refinery.

> It burned at the top of a 250ft stack and we tried all sorts of things to get it to light again. In the end there was only one way of doing it and that was climbing up there with a match and a long piece of wire. A fitter and I went up and did just that. I wouldn't do it today. Just think what could have happened. It could have turned us into a cinder.

When he retired as chairman of British Aerospace in the summer of 1987, Pearce had spent forty-two years in industry, all but ten weeks in management, which must make him something of an authority on the subject. He also underwent the unique experience of being asked by successive governments to take a hand in both the nationalisation of British Aerospace and its subsequent return to the private sector. He has thus learned what qualities are necessary to run a business both under the bureaucratic yoke of government red tape and in the cut and thrust of the world of international competition.

Yet he started his career with a very modest ambition. In his last year at Devonport High School in Plymouth he set himself the aim of finding a job which would earn him £5 a week, because up to that time, his father, a Westcountryman, had never achieved such a princely sum. It seemed to Pearce that the best way to gain his goal was to go into the Civil Service, which was the career that most of the more successful pupils from his school tended to follow. 'I was under pressure from my grandfather to become a teacher and that's the last thing I wanted to be. I knew quite a number of people who had gone into the Civil Service and it seemed a good thing to get into.'

Ironically, fate intervened and he never did make that his career, which is probably just as well, since when he was given the task many years later of steering British Aerospace into the private sector he crossed swords with more than a few civil servants and didn't have a lot of time for them.

The reason he never became one himself is very simple. Germany marched into Poland on his eighteenth birthday and the Civil Service entrance examination he was scheduled to take was cancelled. He was then left with two alternatives – going into the forces or to university. He was advised by his teacher to choose the latter and it was suggested that he should go to Oxford and read chemistry. He applied for, and won, several scholarships, but was particularly attracted to a scholarship in oil engineering that was on offer from Birmingham University.

His teachers at his Plymouth school threw scorn on the idea of going to a redbrick university when he could have chosen Oxford, but he felt a strong pull towards oil engineering and displayed the stubborn streak that was later to characterise his industrial career.

> I read oil engineering which was primarily on the production side and out of a course of thirteen, I was the only one who was interested in the chemical side of it – the refining side. I just loved the idea of being able to use my chemistry in the design side of things. The two things just clicked.

His research work at the university's petroleum warfare department led indirectly to him joining Esso, and within weeks he was faced with one of the many challenges that were to punctuate his rise to the top of the industry. Because of the nature of his studies he was sent to work at the Esso refinery at Fawley. 'I joined the refinery straight from university, never having been anywhere near the place before, and within ten weeks I was actually in charge of my own shift. I was certainly plunged into the deep end.' But he couldn't resist the challenge.

> The way people tackle things is very much the influence of their background and each will achieve things in different ways. I suppose one of the key factors of my whole industrial career has been that if an opportunity comes up, I grab it.

> It could be argued that on occasions I've taken on things which probably I haven't done as well out of financially as I might have done if I'd done something else. But to me the excitement of the job is so much that if something comes along, I don't think twice.

Accepting the refinery job meant that Pearce was able to exceed his £5 a week goal by £1, but it was still a meagre wage for the amount of responsibility he shouldered.

> In 1945 I was paid £6 a week. I had a PhD. I was in charge of a refinery on my own. I was the lowest paid person on the refinery. But the experience I had was fantastic and it didn't take long before my salary was considerably more than that. If I hadn't taken that opportunity I'm sure I would never have done the things I later did in the refinery business.

He had no burning ambition to climb to the upper reaches of management in those early days, however. He recalls vividly being told shortly after he took the job at Fawley refinery that an Esso director would be calling to see him. He had to ask what exactly a director was. But the lessons he learned from those formative years were to stand him in good stead later on when he was to understand what it meant to be a director from first-hand experience.

> When I was put in charge of the start-up at Fawley at the ripe old age of twenty-nine most of my team were people who were twenty years older than I was and being on shift with a lot of operating people taught me the problems and the realisation that I could learn a hell of a lot from them – the realisation that the chap on the shop floor usually knows far more about what's going on than management does.

It also taught him the importance of training. He discovered that learning could be a two-way process. He had a lot to learn about operating methods from the people on the shop floor, but he could also pass on to them the fruits of his university education. He discovered, for example, that laboratory technicians at Fawley were carrying out chemical tests without really understanding what it was they were doing. Pearce offered to fill in the gaps in their knowledge.

> At about 2am I used to go up to the lab. It was a quiet time and I would sit these fellows down for half an hour and take them through what they were doing. They were then prepared to help me. I was green at my job and some of them had been around twenty-five to thirty years doing this sort of work. I learned an awful lot from them.

Pearce is convinced the experience of those early years had important universal lessons of which any young graduate entering industry today ought to take heed.

> I believe any young graduate would get an awful lot of value from working with people on the shop floor. A lot of people today say it's not necessary. I'm afraid we have a lot of people in top management today whose background is such that they don't really get involved with people on the shop floor. I'm talking in the manufacturing sense. Of course a lot of industries today are changing and they don't have as many people on the shop floor anyway and you have many more people who are systems analysts and people like that. But I think it's very important top management should get to know some of the problems those people have too, because if they're not doing it right, the company could be in trouble. But this depends very much on your personality. Some people are very good at it; some people aren't. Some people communicate easily; some don't. In some respects, you have to determine what your strong characteristics are and then use them.

In Pearce's experience it is easy for top management to become remote from the shop floor and lose contact with the centre of operations.

> It's just the pressure you work under. The things you have to do make it progressively more and more difficult for you to really get around and see what's going on in your factories. Take British Aerospace with its twenty different locations.

> Each of them requires a complete day out to go and visit them and it's very difficult to find a complete day because there are so many other things, so many other demands on your time. I would have loved to have spent more time out there where the action is, but it just wasn't practical.

Pearce nevertheless made a point of visiting every single British Aerospace factory at one time or another during his seven years as chairman, some of them more than once.

As Pearce progressed in his career, he found that there was a discernible shift in his management priorities.

> As a refinery supervisor or a supervisor out in one of the British Aerospace factories, you have to get things out that day. There, you're concentrating on getting the job done. It's much more of a hands-on style. The further up the line you get, the longer your time horizon becomes. As a chairman, I didn't have to worry about finding a particular part to put in a piece of kit to make it work. But I did have to worry about whether we were going to have the cash flow in ten years' time to make sure that the parts can be paid for so the chap on the shop floor can stick the thing together.

Pearce considers that one of the main priorities of any top executive should be to develop the managers under him. One of his great disappointments at British Aerospace, he confesses, was that:

> I was not successful in getting the system going as I would really have liked. This was because there are so many old Spanish customs within the company and rigidities of thinking which take a hell of a lot of changing when you're talking about people. Since I've understood what management was about – I suppose that must have been back in the early 1950s – I've had the philosophy that if I go into a job I must do it better than the bloke who's been doing it before me. I've also adopted the philosophy that I must develop somebody to do my job better than I have done it. I don't always succeed in doing that.

Pearce could have done with more than the seven years he had at British Aerospace to achieve the kind of management culture he would have liked to have bequeathed to the company. But he has little hesitation in declaring that his successor as chairman of Esso has done a better job than he was able to achieve. Unashamedly blowing his own trumpet, he also considers that many of the people he selected for management roles in Esso are doing a better job than the people before them. 'They're better trained, better educated. They have many more management techniques, which we didn't have – which we've given them – and of course they've got new ideas coming along as well.'

Pearce's own progression within Esso was a series of the grasped opportunities he talks about enthusiastically. He next became assistant refinery manager and was then promoted to general manager over the head of a friend and colleague who was ten years older. There was a momentary hesitation while he considered the implications, but it was one of the many challenges he couldn't let go. He held the job for five years and became heavily involved in building Esso's Milford Haven refinery and the new Irish refinery. Then one day he was sent for by the refining director and given twenty-four hours to make up his mind about a posting to the United States.

He had been earmarked for senior management and his posting to the US was intended to serve a double purpose. It would give the American parent group a chance to examine his potential at close quarters and at the same time he would be able to undergo some training to prepare him for the more elevated positions he was destined to occupy in future.

Despite the domestic chaos caused from being given such short notice, Pearce again rose to the challenge and had moved with his family to the US within six weeks. But he found that the job that awaited him there was several rungs lower than the job he had been holding down in the UK. He astounded his American masters by demanding that they give him a more worthwhile job or he would be on his way home. He ended up as a departmental head with two other jobs besides. When he returned to the UK he was eventually appointed to the board, but not, as might have been expected, in charge of the refinery side of the business. He was made responsible for marine operations, an area of the business totally new to him.

Pearce pauses for reflection when asked to define the qualities which took him to the top with such apparent ease. But he seems to have no doubts about his answer:

> I think there's got to be determination, consistency, the ability to listen to other people and then make your mind up and stick to it. You can do that in a variety of ways. Some people would do it in a very extrovert way. That's not my way of doing it. I prefer to work quietly behind the scenes. Usually, I know exactly what I want, but it is much better if you can get other people to do it and let them take the credit.
>
> I think I can say that during my career most of the things I've decided ought to be done, I've got done, but I've done them in very different ways to other people and sometimes I've been criticised for not going out and grabbing the headlines. That's not me.

Engineering change through quiet persuasion nevertheless requires clear-cut goals and a strong sense of direction. Pearce lists these as two important qualities for a top manager together with being able to look at a problem and see the two or three key factors. 'You have to say "to hell with the rest of it; that's what you've got to deal with".'

This was precisely the approach Pearce adopted when he was asked by the Conservative Government to become chairman of British Aerospace in 1980 to prepare it for privatisation. Ironically, five years earlier he had been asked by Eric Varley, the Labour Government's Energy Secretary, to serve on the committee for overseeing the nationalisation of the company. He was very clear in his mind, however, about what steps needed to be taken to make the company fit for the private sector. 'One was we had to take an international outlook rather than being a purely British company. The other was trying to find a mechanism to sell more.'

Another example of the ability to see the wood from the trees can be drawn from the time he was asked to take charge of Esso's marine operations.

> When I took on the marine operations every ship had a fifty-four man crew and it seemed to me that this was inefficient,

> so I did a trip on a ship and I came back quite convinced you could actually run a ship with twenty-one men. You also had to maintain things, so I came up with the figure of thirty-one. Everyone in the whole marine department just threw up their hands in horror and told me I was crazy, I didn't know the first thing about ships, the whole marine fleet would fall apart. I also wanted to get the organisation out of London down to Fawley, which is where you have the ships. You can't get many into London!

Again, by exercising his powers of persuasion and sticking to his guns, Pearce's view prevailed and he succeeded in both aims.

> I suppose I've been lucky with my training, having been an engineer. I could look at all these things and say that's just not the right way to do it. It would be better for doing it this way. And you've got to be stubborn. There's no question about it.

Part of the reason Pearce decided to accept the request to head up British Aerospace was that he had been thirty-five years with Esso, eight as chairman. He welcomed the opportunity to move to a British company and he felt in any case that eight years was probably long enough at the top of any major company. That, in his view, is long enough to be able to come up with new ideas and see them implemented. After that, a top executive tends to get stale, in Pearce's opinion, because 'you're seeing the same problems coming up for the second, third or even fourth time and you begin to think you've done it all before. But you haven't because the world's changed.'

He was advised not to overstay his tenure at the head of Esso in unusual circumstances. It happened while he was still managing director of the company in charge of the fleet. A new tanker, the *Esso Northumbria,* the first of its kind, was being launched by Princess Anne at her first public engagement. When the ceremony was over, Pearce was the last to leave the boatyard at Newcastle. He climbed into the bus that was taking him and the company's guests back to the hotel and he sat next to someone he did not recognise in the only seat left vacant.

This person turned to him and asked how old he was. Pearce

said he was forty-nine. The stranger predicted Pearce would be chairman by the time he was fifty. Pearce expressed surprise and said that this was the first he had heard of it. The stranger asked him to promise one thing: 'Don't stay in the job for more than ten years, because you'll get stale. You won't be doing a good thing either for yourself or your company.'

The man who offered this piece of advice turned out to be Lord Cole, who was chairman of Unilever at the time and went on to be chairman of Rolls-Royce and several other major companies. Pearce laughs heartily at the recollection. But he has heeded the advice.

> As a general rule ten years is long enough, but of course it depends on the individual and it depends on the company too. If you are running your own company which you own and have built up from scratch you have a different approach to somebody like myself who's a professional manager. That's what I am, let's face it. It doesn't matter whether I like it or not; it's a fact of life. I didn't own the companies I worked for. I've got a few shares in British Aerospace, but nobody would notice if I sold them all.

Pearce believes a professional manager can be equally successful at running a variety of companies, but he needs to be selective about the switches he makes.

> I could switch from oil, which has a chemical background, to the chemical industry. I think I could go to the food industry or to the brewing industry. I'm an engineer by training, so I could move into something like British Aerospace. But could I switch to be chairman of Burtons, for example? That's a very different sort of activity. It's possible but it would not be a very natural switch.

Pearce's switch to British Aerospace was helped by the fact that he had been a non-executive director of the aerospace company for three years prior to the move. But being a nationalised company the chairman's salary was fixed and the £80,000 annual remuneration Pearce was receiving as chairman of Esso was cut in half overnight. He did have the advantage, however, of pursuing a single specific goal – that of taking the company through privatisation. Although he had helped to set up British Aerospace as a nationalised company, he was convinced it could not take on the huge rival plane-makers in the United States unless it was unfettered from government control.

> Basically, my objective was to ensure that British Aerospace stayed in business somehow. I had agreed with the necessity of BAC and Hawker Siddeley being put together in one company, but having a nationalised company that involved a lot of civil servants and politicians was a ghastly inefficient way of doing things. A lot of people involved, a number of ministers and most of the civil servants, were delightful people, very charming people, but they weren't trained to run an organisation. They didn't think in the right way. It was unfair to them, quite frankly.

There were quite a few battles before Pearce got British Aerospace on the road to privatisation, particularly with civil servants and 'officials who were not really responsible, but tended to sit on the sidelines criticising and always coming up with a reason why you couldn't do anything.'

Positive thinking is another cause Pearce has always tried to promote.

> If you produce a proposal, the first thing a lot of British engineers will do is tell you what's wrong with it. That, I regret, is a British characteristic. I wish they would adopt the positive principle of looking at something and seeing the good in it – seeing how it can be improved by building up the positive aspects. The British engineer tends to look at something and knock it down.

Pearce also met with a considerable degree of resistance from within British Aerospace in his efforts to steer it through privatisation.

> There were individual factory loyalties and there were divisional loyalties and it had been a pretty cosy relationship between the organisation and the Ministry of Defence. So

> why destroy it? It's very important for a chairman or chief executive to recognise that the world is going to change. A lot of people just think by definition the world is going to carry on as it is today, but it doesn't. You've got to try and guess what's going to happen in three, four or five years' time.

The chairman of a company like British Aerospace has to anticipate change on a global scale. He has to look at everything from an international perspective. For Pearce, with his strong belief in personal contacts, that has meant a lot of travel to different parts of the world. It has also meant visiting customers worldwide, but he admits that his greatest pleasure came from meeting the company's own employees around the globe.

> I had to meet customers and politicians and people like that, but the greatest thrill for me is meeting our own people, letting them know we hadn't forgotten them and getting ideas from them, hearing what they think about the company and things like that. That involved a fair amount of travel. I don't enjoy getting from point A to point B. The last place I want to go to is an airport.

Getting the right balance in life is important to Pearce. He has always been careful to balance his busy executive life with a strong interest in extramural activities. He has been particularly keen on educational pursuits. He is pro-chancellor of the University of Surrey and chairman of the trustees of the Science Museum in South Kensington. He believes that industrialists have a lot to offer academic institutions in helping them to manage their resources.

> All the universities today are under enormous pressure financially. The government's giving them less and less to work with. It's a question of giving them help in areas where they may not traditionally have had expertise. As far as the Science Museum is concerned it's a question of helping it with the whole game of raising finance and all the other things they have to do. One of the things museums are going to have to do in future is take over their buildings.

> Curators are not used to coping with that. They don't have a clue what maintenance of buildings is all about. The PSA has always done it in the past. Now they've got to do it for themselves. They don't know where to start.

Pearce has found that his involvement in so many outside bodies has helped to broaden his knowledge and outlook. In his Esso days he was invited to join the board of Williams & Glyn. He found that it opened a window on the City that he would otherwise never have had. It meant he could go and talk to the governor of the Bank of England and the chairmen of any of the clearing banks whenever he felt the need. When he was approached to run British Aerospace the government insisted he should give up the directorship of W&G, but Pearce, displaying his usual resolve, wouldn't hear of it. He felt the contact was so invaluable that he was prepared to turn down the job at the head of one of the UK's premier blue-chip companies if it meant making such a sacrifice.

Pearce is not convinced that it is any tougher to be a top executive today than in the past, despite the faster pace and greater complexity of modern business activities.

> You've got to deal with different problems, there's no question about that. They're on a worldwide scale rather than a national scale, but you have to recognise that there are only so many hours in the day in which you can be efficient. Therefore you've got to be selective in what you do and you've got to be the right person to deal with those things, of course. And you have to be updated periodically, more so than in the past.

Nor does Pearce believe up-and-coming managers should be put off by the apparent decline in moral standards of business. He believes standards have only slipped in the case of a few companies, but that the press tends to seize on these examples and blow them up out of all proportion. He asserts that in the majority of businesses the moral standards have improved very significantly.

> But the media only pick out the failures, because that's what

> we as readers want to read. You can blame the media, but really you ought to blame the readers. No matter where you are, there are always a few black sheep. The snag today is that those black sheep will create much bigger problems than they could in the past.

What specific advice would Pearce pass on to the next generation of senior executives?

> Make damn sure you've got the right people in the right place, so they do the work rather than you. You've got to concentrate on financial control, on your customer and on your people. These are the three main areas.

Anita Roddick

Born: Littlehampton, Sussex, 1942.
Educated: Worthing High School for Girls; Bath College of Education.

Anita Roddick is managing director of The Body Shop International plc, a group of more than three hundred cosmetic shops in thirty-three countries, stretching from the Arctic Circle to Australia. The company claims to have a larger presence abroad than any other British retailer, trading in thirteen different languages.

Roddick experienced her first taste of trading as a child while serving in the family café in Littlehampton in Sussex, which is now the centre of her worldwide retailing empire. Before going into the cosmetic business she was a teacher, and worked for the United Nations in Geneva. It was while travelling around the world for the UN that she first became impressed with the simple forms of cosmetics made from natural ingredients used by remote communities.

When she returned to the UK, however, she entered into the restaurant and hotel business with her husband Gordon. Looking for a less demanding occupation, she opened the first Body Shop in a tiny premises in a back street of Brighton in 1976, selling fifteen different products in plastic bottles with hand-written labels. She set up the business with a £4,000 bank loan and shortage of capital persuaded her to expand through franchising. The decision set in motion a chain reaction that was to become an international phenomenon – hundreds of shops, all a mirror image of her original concept no matter where in the world they are located.

The Body Shop went public in 1984 and the company's shares have consistently dazzled City analysts with their high performance. As one leading business magazine put it: 'Body Shop's star in the City is not so much rising as super-glued to the roof of the firmament.' The same magazine declared The Body Shop the second fastest growing medium-sized business in Britain in a survey of two hundred firms. This is particularly remarkable when it is considered that Roddick has made no acquisitions and has no major plans for diversification.

She was awarded the OBE in the 1988 New Year's Honours List.

Anita Roddick has made a virtue of flying in the face of business convention. She seems to thrive on heretical statements and swimming against the tide: 'I look at what the cosmetic trade is doing and walk in the opposite direction,' she declares with the kind of outspoken defiance that has made her a retailing legend in the decade it took her to turn The Body Shop into a worldwide phenomenon.

She once summed up to a gathering of marketing specialists the extent of her success, which earned The Body Shop the award of business of the year in 1987:

> We produce over three hundred products in well over three hundred shops from the Arctic Circle to Adelaide, covering thirty-one countries and thirteen languages, without once diluting our image. We've done this with humour, intelligence, a sense of joy, magic and fun, which have always been our essential ingredients.

In achieving this remarkable success, Roddick has always been scornful of traditional business credos. She refuses to be part of the general cosmetic industry hype. She will make no extravagant claims for her skin- and hair-care products, all derived from natural ingredients. There is no room in her vocabulary for terms like 'nourishing cream', because 'only food nourishes'. She has never had to advertise any of her products because 'the shops and the product are the best advertisement'. Her success speaks for itself. She has never hired anyone with a business-school education, because she believes such people are too rigid in their outlook. She has set up her own training school because she found conventional training schemes offered no scope for the kind of message she wants to get across. She has even formed her own film and video group because she finds most training films 'a yawn a minute'.

She has trodden her own distinctive path guided by her mission to make The Body Shop 'the most honest cosmetic company in the world' because she could find no shining example in the retailing industry from which to draw inspiration.

> For me there are no modern-day heroes in the retailing world. I have come across not one company which incorporates the pursuit of honest profits with social awareness, which provides a vision for themselves and their workers. I have met no retailing captain of industry who makes my blood sing.
>
> Retailing itself has taught me nothing. I see tired executives in tired systems. These huge corporations are dying of boredom caused by the inertia of giantism.

This is a fate Roddick has avoided by operating most of her shops under a franchise system. It was a route she chose originally because she did not have enough capital to expand at the rate business demanded. But she has no intention of changing course now as she believes that, run as separate entities, the shops remain manageable and provide a strong incentive to succeed for the franchisees.

She nevertheless keeps a tight control on the products, the shop displays, training and the operating style of the shops. There is, for example, an unwritten clause insisting that franchisees must agree to adopt a community project. In this way, all the shops reflect Roddick's concern for the environment and her insistence that private wealth should be used for public good.

It is all part of Roddick's determination to imbue retailing with a higher status in society. This is something she feels strongly about and she tends to become even more animated than usual when trying to articulate her philosophy. A torrent of words pour out as thoughts race around in her head, vying with each other for verbal expression. She basically lays the blame for the low status retailing enjoys today at the door of the education system. A former teacher, she speaks with some authority on the subject.

> Some of the most important social changes and some of the greatest philanthropists in the last century were in the field of retailing and yet they are not our heroes. It's not part of our culture; it's not written up in the history books. One of the reasons is that people in this country don't value labour. They talk about it as an expenditure and not as an investment. They are always quibbling about the amount they are prepared to pay their staff while drawing enormous salaries for themselves. People forget that their staff are their front-line consumers.

Roddick cossets her staff. They get free samples because their opinions about the products are highly valued. There's a suggestion box at every till. They are also given share options. Training includes courses in sociology and in urban survival. She justifies this by pointing out that there are three thousand young women working in town centres around the country, whose welfare is paramount to her. She even invites AIDS sufferers to come and talk to them.

What Roddick is at most pains to demonstrate is that honesty and commercialism can make compatible bedfellows. Indeed, she would argue that her forthright and uncompromising approach is a vital element of her success.

> The cosmetic industry is bizarre because it is run by men who create needs that don't exist, making women feel incredibly dissatisfied with their bodies. They have this extraordinary belief that all women want is hope and promise. They've got this absolute obsession with not telling the truth, which is bizarre because some of the products they make are actually good. But to me it's innately dishonest to make claims that a cream that is basically oil and water is going to take grief and stress and fifty years of living in the sun off your face. It's nonsense.

Roddick attributes her entrepreneurial flair and her individualism to her upbringing. She was one of four children born to Italian immigrants. She helped in the family café at the Sussex seaside resort of Littlehampton, which is still the base for her worldwide empire of retailing outlets. She has fond memories of the café, which was a popular meeting place for a large number of local children. 'We had the first juke-box in the town after the war, the first nickerbocker glories and the first Pepsi-Colas.' But it wasn't an easy life, particularly as her father died while she was still quite young.

> Coming from a first-generation immigrant family there was a strongly defined work ethic and after my father died heavy responsibility was thrust upon us. All of the children had to contribute and to some extent we lost our childhood. We didn't have time to play on the beach or in the streets with the other kids.
>
> I didn't know it then but I was receiving subliminal training for later business life. I was always surrounded by strong images – the image of the café, how it looked and the service it provided. We kids either had to serve behind the ice-cream counter or wait on the tables. One of the most important aspects is that we saw ourselves as town traders - that magical area where buyer and seller come together.
>
> One of the bizarre things I find today is that England doesn't really like traders. They're very happy with manufacturing, but the selling of the product and the trading is not quite the right thing to do. They think it's a bit *infra dig*.

But Roddick did not immediately turn her trading experience into entrepreneurial endeavour when she grew up. Typical of immigrants, her parents were anxious that she should do better than they and persuaded her to take up teaching as a profession. Roddick did not offer any resistance, because at the time she was a frustrated actress and she felt teaching English and history to a class of forty kids at a local secondary school was the next best thing to acting.

> It wasn't a hardship because good teaching is theatre. I learned how to create atmosphere so that the classroom was a visual delight. I always did things differently. Friday afternoons I did a course in aesthetics and I was allowed to paint the classroom – an old Nissen hut – black and red. I couldn't believe that anyone could live their life and not be surrounded by brilliant objects and colours. I always taught

> my history lessons with the most relevant music. So if we were talking about the Middle Ages we had Gregorian chants, or if we were doing the First World War we had First-world-war songs. Everywhere I went my individuality was encouraged.

Roddick is convinced her own schooling was also influential in forming her attitudes to life and the business world. She failed her eleven-plus and ended up at a local secondary modern school, which turned out to be a blessing in disguise. It was the first secondary modern school in the area to introduce O-level courses and the young Roddick was one of twenty girls specially selected to participate in the experiment. 'So right from an early age I was told I was special. I had the best schooling in the world. It was magic.'

Prior to becoming a teacher, Roddick decided she wanted to see something of the world. 'I thought the intelligent thing to do was to go away and work for two years and then come back and teach. Where do you go in the 1960s? You go to Paris to suffer.' She worked in the Paris office of the New York *Herald Tribune* for a while and later she went to Switzerland to work for the International Labour Office of the United Nations. Her confidence and conviction that she was somebody special served her well when she applied for the UN job. Although she had never had any secretarial training, she had the nerve to apply for one of the most eagerly sought-after positions in Europe. Asked what her typing speed was, she bluntly replied: 'Hit and miss and the use of a rubber.' She gave a similarly flippant answer when inquiries were made about her shorthand skills: 'Longhand and memory,' was her answer. 'Then I said what I *can* do – organise, put twenty-four hours in a day and I'm energetic. I just sold myself.'

Even at that early stage in her career, Roddick knew she was different and she cultivated it. She finds it hard to explain why, but ponders that it may have something to do with the religious faith she grew up with.

> It was a sort of Catholic stab against death, I suppose. You try to defy death all the time when you've had a Catholic upbringing, because it's just so awful. I suppose it's striving

> for immortality, just being different, making your mark. I lived in a town called Littlehampton. All it needed was a bit of tumbleweed to make it seem more deserted than it really was and I used to just fight against that dissatisfaction. My friends at sixteen were getting married or getting pregnant. I just wanted something more than that.

It was while travelling around the world that the seeds of her future calling were first sown. Courtesy of the UN, which paid her a handsome tax-free salary, she travelled widely, visiting exotic spots like Polynesia, Mauritius and the New Hebrides. She spent time with remote island communities and observed the simple but effective way they lived their lives. 'I just lived as they did and watched how they groomed themselves without any cosmetic aids. Their skin was wonderful and their hair beautifully clean.' She watched Polynesians scoop up untreated cocoa butter and apply it directly to their skins and felt the smooth texture the skin consequently acquired. Today, Roddick spends about two months a year travelling the world, picking up tips about natural ingredients to go into her products. Cocoa butter is now an important ingredient in her skin-care products, for example. She has also observed Sri Lankans using pineapple as a skin cleanser and later discovered that the natural enzymes present in the fruit act on the skin to remove dead cells, making it an effective cleanser.

> We can learn from women in other societies. They know that these well-tried and tested ways work, and do not need a scientist or advertising agency to sell them. You only have to look at what they use. Very often it is a plant which grows readily at hand. There are more than 200,00 known plant species in the world and it is said we have learned to use only 2,500 of them. It is the marriage of traditional wisdom and knowledge of raw ingredients with modern research that makes The Body Shop products innovative and effective.

But the idea for The Body Shop did not take root immediately. By the time she returned from travelling the world, she was in her mid-twenties. She fell in love, married and opened a restaurant with her husband Gordon. Looking back on it, Roddick believes that too was a good training ground for future developments.

> Terence Conran once said to me: 'the reason why you and I do things well is because we had our apprenticeship in restaurants,' and I actually think that's a very valid point, because you've got twenty planks to the one function of actually serving food. You've got to order, you've got to prepare, you've got to have the right environment – the character of the place – and you've got to sell what you're offering, for example.

The original plan was that Anita would do the cooking and her husband would serve the customers, but she did not enjoy being behind the scenes and eventually taught Gordon to be a fine cook while she spent her time out front chatting up the customers. After two years, however, Gordon too got the wanderlust urge and planned a horse-back ride from South America to New York that would take him two years. Anita encouraged him to go and decided that while he was away, running a shop would be a less demanding occupation than working all hours in a restaurant. It had occurred to her that most products came in a variety of sizes and offered a wide choice, but she felt the cosmetic trade was too dictatorial about what the customer should buy. She envisaged a shop where cleansing lotions would be displayed in simple bottles of all shapes and sizes and which would contain the natural ingredients she had come across during her trips to remote communities.

Personal experience, Roddick maintains, is the best market research there is.

> You can't just pull ideas out of the air. You've got to find out what irritates you, annoys you to death and then translate that into a business. What irritates me about going shopping in any supermarket is having to bag my own goods up. Why isn't there somebody there to bag them for me and create a service?

Starting with a bank loan of £4,000, Roddick had no time to sit down in the early years and draw up a grandiose mission of what her organisation should set out to achieve. The first, and crucial, goal was survival.

> Reality says that if you set up a store and you're under-capitalised, you're going to go bust. The reason you do it usually is because if you don't succeed you're not going to eat. So you put in all the hours God gives you. You pray that you'll make enough to pay the rates and the petrol for the car. That's your apprenticeship. My apprenticeship was in a shop for a year working and adapting and changing and getting an understanding of it all. Also, learning to be obsessive about detail. It's the detail that matters.

The success of The Body Shop grew out of an almost naïve belief in herself and sheer hard work.

> Having been told I was special from a very young age, you believe everything is possible, but I also knew that you got nothing unless you worked hard. We were protected by not really knowing the risks. We worked hard, therefore we survived. We didn't know what the risk factors were. We didn't have any understanding of the business colleges. In fact, I would suggest that anybody who has one ounce of individuality should never go to a business school – and I've said this often at Cranfield and London – because you're structured by academics who measure you in the science of business. They use a business language that is so predictable and going out and doing it is not part of the course.

Lack of academic training does not appear to have been a handicap for Roddick. The Body Shop expanded rapidly under the franchise system. Roddick merely called it 'self-financing', because she didn't have the capital to do it any other way. 'We just went in and did everything for everybody. We helped with putting up the shelves and we filled all the bottles in each shop. Everyone did their own labelling.'

As a result of this approach, a strong camaraderie developed between the Roddicks and the franchisees they selected to help spread their business philosophy. They found themselves working alongside like-minded young people with similar values to their own. Roddick describes herself and her husband as 'children of the 1960s'. They had both been ardent followers of such causes as Shelter, Freedom from Hunger and the Campaign for Nuclear Disarmament, the popular issues of the day for caring people with deep moral convictions. As her business empire grew, Roddick was left with little time to participate actively in such environmental causes as Friends of the Earth and Greenpeace, with which her own convictions were closely aligned. But she made certain that her great concern for environmental issues were built into her business philosophy.

For example, The Body Shop was the first company in Britain to use jojoba oil, which is obtained from a desert plant, in cosmetics. The plant oil closely resembles sperm-whale oil, which has been used in cosmetics for many years. Her way of supporting Greenpeace's campaign to save the whale was to demonstrate that there are always substitutes to be found in nature and that there is no commercial excuse for hunting an endangered species out of existence. There are, in fact, other powerful reasons for making jojoba a universal substitute for whale oil. It can be grown on some of the poorest land in the world, which is totally unsuitable for conventional crops, and in regions where people have no work and are living in poverty. Roddick has pledged herself and her organisation to 'increasing public awareness of the qualities of jojoba oil and to lead the way by using it extensively, so helping both people and whales.'

This enlightened approach came as a natural product of Roddick's values and her philosophy of life. It wasn't until she had successfully launched The Body Shop on to the Unlisted Securities Market that she began to examine the direction in which the business was going and to start articulating its mission in a definitive way. She suddenly realised she had passed from the survival phase to a phase where she could see that The Body Shop had become a retailing institution that was going from strength to strength. This left her asking herself how she should direct her success and what her responsibilities to society were.

> Instead of letting our success lead us into a fat-cat mentality, it led us much more strongly and much faster into a mentality of asking what are we going to do with it. Everybody's shop was making a lot of money and we just couldn't bear the

> thought of us all getting like the rest of the industry. I was learning very fast to walk in the opposite direction. There was just one yardstick. Whatever the cosmetics industry was doing, do the opposite. It worked well.

One of the main outcomes of all this introspection was the setting up of an environmental and communities department to translate Roddick's beliefs and concerns into practical projects. The Body Shop as a group joined Friends of the Earth and pursued such policies as using recycled paper for packaging. But more importantly, as far as Roddick is concerned, each franchised outlet is required to take on a community project in its area, which she believes gives the young women in the organisation additional status and helps them to realise that everybody has the ability to change the world for the better. But none of the employees are expected to take on extra duties after a hard day in the shop. All the projects are undertaken within working hours. Each franchisee decides their own project. There is no question of coercion.

But Roddick sees her expanding retailing network as a means to spread her own deep beliefs about the environment and Third World issues, educating both employees and customers. She sees the whole process as a self-perpetuating cycle. Ingredients obtained from the Third World, providing work and sustenance to underprivileged societies, go into products which are sold to the more fortunate, the profits of which go into her educational programme aimed at making people more aware of the critical issues of our times.

> We're the only company I know that puts issues like acid rain, waste and pollution as shop-window issues to educate our customers. In a way, we've almost come full circle back to what I was trained to do, which is teaching. We have half a million kids coming into our shops every week. Just to sell them a product without educating them to challenge and to care about the ingredients that go into those products would be wrong. They should be constantly asking why a bottle is the shape it is and whether the ingredients come from a whale or from a natural substance of which there is great abundance. The cosmetics industry

is an irrelevant industry. It is not a life and death industry, so it is a joyous task to create more relevancy.

Typical of the kind of community projects The Body Shop undertakes is one run in collaboration with the Brighton Health Authority. Part-time workers, recruited through the Manpower Services Commission, are being trained to provide a regular massage service for elderly and psychiatric patients. It has also become involved in the Work-out scheme in London, which aims to help the young unemployed take an active approach to life. Body Shop staff adopt a young unemployed person on a one-to-one basis, helping with job applications, for example. Attempts are also being made to set up community-run Body Shops in inner urban areas, such as Brixton.

Roddick's determination to use private profit for public good has now reached some of the remotest parts of the world. She has launched a number of Third World projects, which she often discovers during her two months abroad each year. One of her latest projects is to set up a paper-making plant in Nepal. The paper will be processed from pineapple and banana leaves, under the initial guidance of a Canadian crafts specialist. Roddick plans to use the paper so produced for wrapping Body Shop products. There's a similar plan to make paper from water hyacinth in Bangladesh. The water hyacinth grows in profusion and tends to choke up the local rivers. So the project will have the double benefit of clearing the rivers and at the same time creating a saleable product.

In southern India The Body Shop has provided the means to set up a boys' town for destitute youngsters. They are taught rural crafts and how to make products, such as foot rollers and Christmas cards, which are sold in The Body Shops. The money from the sale of the products is put into a trust fund, so that when the youngsters leave at the age of sixteen to make their own way in the world they have the means to purchase a flock of sheep or a horse and cart, giving them a vital start in whatever activity they take up. Any additional revenue goes into funding more boys' towns. So far three thousand jobs have been created under the scheme.

Roddick has never found that her commercial and philanthropic interests clash. She refused to listen to the Jeremiahs who predicted she would have to change her operating style once her company came under the scrutiny of the Stock Exchange.

> I have learned a lot in the last few years. There are a hell of a lot of myths perpetrated in this industry. They say when you go on to the Stock Market you should be worried because you can lose your strength. It's just not true. If you're doing well, the Stock Market leaves you alone and what's even better, if you're doing terrifically well, as we are, they listen to you. They spend more and more time trying to study how we work and how we do things. The second myth says that the bigger you get, the less communication you have. That's nonsense. We've invested an enormous amount in communications at all levels – our training school, a newsletter, videos, and so on – and it works.

Nor is Roddick fearful that she will be unable to ensure that the most suitable people are recruited to join The Body Shop as it continues to grow at such a fast pace. She points out that there are five thousand people on the waiting list wanting to take up a Body Shop franchise and that it takes three years before any of them succeed. 'Unless you're absolutely obsessed you don't get a look in.' Applicants also have to undergo strict vetting, which includes an offbeat questionnaire. Roddick calls it the Marcel Proust questionnaire and it asks such unlikely questions as: How would you like to die? What's your favourite flower? Who's your heroine in history or who's your hero in poetry? Roddick claims that the answers to such bizarre questions tend to be very revealing and she can usually judge whether an applicant is going to be somebody who is on her wavelength and with whom she can comfortably work.

In fact, Roddick has managed to achieve an astonishing uniformity with her worldwide network of shops. Wherever you are, each is a mirror image of all the others.

> We've got stores in the Arctic Circle, we've got shops literally in the desert in the Middle East and we've got them in Hong Kong and Singapore and they're all the same – and they all work. I think the interesting fact is we're not seen

> as an English company. We're seen as cross-cultural with a product range with international ingredients.

Roddick has also resisted suggestions that she should diversify into other quite different product lines such as clothing and leisure centres. 'All I want to do is to do what I'm doing, but do it better.'

The main pleasure Roddick derives from her success is,

> the ability to effect change for the better. There's power in money, but it's not often been utilised for good. I've never seen private greed translate to public benefit ever. There are two things I work on now. Because we're successful, we're listened to. Because we're humane, we're watched – and they're still watching us because they can't believe that you can develop one without losing the other. All you have to do is commit yourself to it. The one thing I can't stand is cynicism. It's so soulless and inert. It changes nothing; it's a disease of the old.

Private wealth certainly doesn't appear to have been translated into personal greed where Roddick is concerned. She rarely indulges herself. The pace of business growth is such that she finds very few spare moments for leisure-time activities. 'For me work is more fun than fun and the one thing I was never trained for was leisure.' What she most relishes about no longer having to worry about where the money to pay the rates is coming from is that it gives her the freedom to be creative. 'Money is never the motivator,' she insists.

Peter de Savary

Born: Burnham on Crouch, Essex, 1944.
Educated: Charterhouse Public School.

At the age of sixteen, Peter de Savary set out for Canada, where he worked as a salesman and later established a baby-sitting business. He returned to Britain at the age of twenty-one and went to work as production manager in his father's furniture business. After being refused a salary rise, he again set out to make his fortune abroad. His travels took him to West Africa, South America and the Middle East. While in Nigeria, he saw opportunities for trading in oil and building products. He became a middleman, providing a trading link between Nigeria, as it developed on the back of its oil boom, and the outside world.

Later, in 1977, he discovered similar opportunities in the Middle East, particularly in Kuwait. He became a director of a Kuwait- and London-based bank.

In 1981, he invested in a property just off London's St James's Street which he turned into the first of what was to become a chain of luxurious clubs that stretch from Antigua to Paris. He paid £15m for a magnificent town château in Paris to create the third St James's Club. The clubs were subsequently sold to the Norfolk Capital Hotel Group with de Savary remaining involved as president. In 1987 he paid £90m to acquire Aspinall's, the gaming club which occupies a prime site in central London.

In the same year he bought a majority stake in Alfred Walker, a barely profitable Midlands-based property group, which grew by two thousand per cent in the first year of the new ownership to a capital value of £125m. Renamed LandLeisure, the company was the vehicle de Savary used to buy Land's End, the famous Cornish beauty spot, for just under £7m, with the intention of upgrading the tourist facilities there.

In November 1988 LandLeisure was sold for £180m to the Leisure Investments group run by Stephen and James Forsyth, the owners of a string of popular London restaurants. But de Savary retained his interests in Land's End and a £35m marina and property development in Falmouth.

De Savary wanted to focus his energies on running Highland Participants, the oil and exploration group he also bought in 1987 and which he used as a vehicle to acquire Falmouth Docks.

Falmouth is the base for his £10m challenge for the America's Cup, international yacht racing's most prestigious prize. The bid is sponsored by Blue Arrow, the world's largest employment services group. De Savary made his first bid for the America's Cup in 1983 with a yacht called Victory. *He lost out to Alan Bond's winning entry, but came closer to winning than any Englishman for fifty years.*

He lives in a seventy-two roomed Tudor mansion called Littlecote in the Berkshire countryside, for which he paid around £7m and which he has turned into a popular tourist attraction.

The story goes that Peter de Savary bought Land's End for just under £7m on little more than a whim. He took friends to see Cornwall's bleakest and most famous landmark in 1987 and was so appalled by the inadequate tourist facilities he found there that he decided something had to be done about them. The multi-millionaire tycoon insists that the reasons behind the investment go deeper than that. But it is typical of de Savary that once he sees a challenge he has to go for it and usually, once he has made up his mind to tackle a new project, money doesn't stand in his way.

There has been no shortage of challenges for de Savary to take on in the Westcountry. Apart from acquiring Land's End, he has also bought a controlling interest in Falmouth Docks, which have been struggling for years since the shipping industry was hit by a world recession. The Falmouth Ship Repair yard used to employ 4,500 men, but at the time de Savary took control of it in 1987 it was finding it hard to keep a tenth of that number in work. But the stocky, dark-bearded tycoon tends to accentuate the positive rather than dwell on the negative. Falmouth has long been regarded as one of the world's last great unexploited natural harbours and de Savary is also involved in plans for a container port there and for a £35m redevelopment of the waterfront, including a marina. He also sees Falmouth as an ideal base from which to launch his challenge for the America's Cup, international yacht racing's most prestigious prize.

Both the investment in Falmouth and in Land's End are the sort of gambles a freewheeling entrepreneur like de Savary finds irresistible. He loves to talk about the pioneering spirit and, as he puts it, 'the thrill of the chase', drawing an inescapable comparison between his business and yachting aspirations. De Savary sees the entrepreneur playing a very different role to that of the 'caretaker' professional managers who oversee such industrial giants as GEC, ICI and Rolls-Royce. But he regards the entrepreneur and the professional manager as interdependent. He does not believe the entrepreneur could operate successfully without the supporting fabric of established industry, even though in many ways he is the antithesis of everything conventional business stands for.

> The entrepreneur exists out of being essentially in the right place at the right time, dealing with the right people and doing the right thing in terms of responding to opportunity very quickly, very flexibly within the umbrella of the established companies. An entrepreneur, quite differently from established businesses, does not have a long-term strategy, is not able to forecast accurately his growth and his progression – where he will be in five years or even perhaps one year. It is not a snowball that is planned to roll along at a certain rate and get bigger and better, which is what an established business does.
>
> If you're in the shipping business you have five ships today and you have a plan to have eight ships next year, fourteen ships the year after and to trade the smaller ships for bigger ones. Traditional businesses are very orderly in their forecasts and their progression and their strategy. An entrepreneur needs those established houses in order that he can fill in the irregularities of a planned system, because the majority of businesses are all planning themselves on even keels and don't want the ups and downs. The entrepreneur fills the need when in fact those peaks and troughs occur. He thrives on them. He picks up the slack or he sucks out the surplus of any given situation at any given time.

De Savary's business interests in the Westcountry are a good example of how an entrepreneur should be flexible enough to switch from one kind of transaction to a very different one and cope with them equally well. Operating Land's End as a successful tourist attraction is a very different kettle of fish from running a ship-repair yard like Falmouth.

> An entrepreneur is not usually tied to any one industrial sector. He's normally fleet of foot. He's normally, if he's successful, supported by a fairly large staff of people who understand him and are specialists in given areas. I, for instance, have specialists in manufacturing, trade unions and labour relations and marketing and all that side of things, and I have other specialists who are experts in creativity, who know how to analyse what the British public or tourist at large wants in the way of amusement. You have to know how to interpret that creatively, putting it together practically into a product. I have other people who understand the service side; you've got to present that and exhibit it very well. These different types of businesses require the skill of the entrepreneur to make them happen, to identify them and fill the need in the market.

The entrepreneur survives, in de Savary's view, by knowing a lot of people and having a high degree of credibility, because generally speaking he does not have any wares to sell.

> The chairman of Rolls-Royce is judged on the quality of the engine and the success of the sales of the engine. He has an engine to show people. GEC has products to show people. The entrepreneur rarely has a product that he can say is his product. By his very nature, the degree of credibility and acceptability an entrepreneur needs is much higher than that needed by the chairman of a major manufacturing company.

A good example is de Savary's acquisition of Land's End. His plans for it were quickly endorsed by the local community and the authorities because they judged his credibility to be such that he and his experts would take the right steps to preserve its natural beauty while at the same time making it more appealing to the tourist; similarly with Falmouth Docks.

> The faith in my ability to make a success of Falmouth does not stem from the fact that I have been the world's most successful ship-repair yard operator for twenty years or that I have twenty-five other shipyards to my credit. It's my credibility and the standards that I can project and the ideas and the wherewithal to carry them out.

De Savary stresses that the true entrepreneur should not be confused with a broker.

> There's a big difference between an entrepreneurial principal and an entrepreneurial broker. The entrepreneurial principal puts his money where his mouth is. The entrepreneurial broker is just trying to carve a slice for himself in the middle between two parties. People have to believe in the entrepreneur. They accept a lot of it on face value, whereas the established industrial leaders have those industries behind them. If you're the chairman of British Steel you have all of British Steel behind you as your calling card. The entrepreneur has his ideas, his initiatives and his recognition of a need in a given market place at a given time. Cornwall is a classic example of that. Cornwall is in desperate need in its peaks and troughs of the tourism industry. It is currently in the depths of a trough. It has never been worse since the war. The numbers of tourists in Cornwall are falling every year; they fell last year; they fell the year before and the year before that. That, to an entrepreneurial principal, is a window of opportunity. It naturally means he has to be a much bigger risk-taker than a caretaker manager. He has to be able to analyse the risks and the rewards and the ratio between the two. An entrepreneur survives by getting the odds right on the risk-reward ratios. That's what he has to be good at. He needs an enormous amount of experience to draw on. You just have to look at the things I've been involved in. They range from avocado farms in California to logs in Brazil, to hotels in Egypt, oil in the Middle East, ships in Africa to pit props in Turkey to coal from Romania. You get to know a

lot of people. You listen a lot, you talk a lot, you read a lot and you gain a broad base of knowledge. That's what you use when you measure the risk and anticipate the reward.

But even with his vast experience, de Savary admits that there are always a number of imponderables when it comes to taking on something like the Falmouth Ship Repair yard. Deciding whether or not to go ahead with such a project is a question of drawing up a balance sheet of risks and rewards in order to calculate the probability of success.

If it was easy and something you could write down and give to other people, everyone would be doing it. It's not an exact science. It's very inexact. It is to a large degree based on hunch and you have to examine the fundamentals to get to that hunch. For example, if you wished to create the existing facilities at Falmouth Docks it would cost upwards of £200m. That's a plus. Falmouth is located thirteen and a half miles from one of the busiest shipping lanes in the world. There is nowhere else in north-west Europe that is within that proximity. That is a unique advantage. Falmouth is the third largest natural harbour probably in the world and we are able to bring in vast ships there. The location, the geographics of it are such that the weather rarely makes it an unsafe harbour; another plus. We do a balance sheet in our minds of all the pluses and then you've got to look at the negatives.

The ship-repair industry is in the doldrums. It is not an easy business. The ship-repair industry in Europe receives subsidies; there are no subsidies in England for ship-repairers. We are in competition with a certain number of yards in England; there probably isn't enough work to go round. That's another negative. On the other hand, a plus is that in our view the next three or four years will see an increase in shipping activity; we think the freight rates will increase over the next three or four years. There will be more traffic; more demand for ships. The effect of that is that in the past seven years very few ships have been built. The amount of new ships that have been built is very low because the market has been bad. That means the owners will have to keep fixing up their old ships to take advantage of the strengthening market. That means they're going to need ship repairers.

You go through all this and you build up a balance sheet of the pluses and minuses and you review it all and weigh it up. You probably talk to some people you respect. You put your thinking cap on and at the end of the day you examine the risk-reward ratio and you consider the downside. I'm paying X, I'm going to invest Y; if it all fails what can I salvage from the pot? I'm not going to lose all my money. How much can I lose? Can I afford to lose that much? What are the potential profits – the upside of it all?

De Savary drew up a similar risk-reward balance sheet before deciding to buy Land's End.

When we looked at Land's End, we asked ourselves: do we have to sell it as a destination? Millions and millions of people are already going to the Westcountry. Nobody is coming to Land's End just to see Land's End. What we have to convince them is that having come to the Westcountry, they should make a point of going to Land's End. You've got a lot of hotels and B&Bs, caravan and camping sites in the Westcountry where we can display our advertising material. You build up a picture as to whether you think you can attract the minimum number of people your figures tell you that you need at Land's End to make it a viable proposition.

De Savary has a special affection for the Westcountry. He grew up in Cornwall and has spent a third of his life in the region. But he had to go much further afield to make his fortune. He left school just before his sixteenth birthday, at the request of his headmaster, with only one 'O' level (in scripture). This was probably the best motivation to succeed that he could have had. 'I was a dismal failure at school. That didn't please me. But making money has never been the priority. I think achieving things that are worthwhile is the priority and I set out to prove that I could do something successfully.'

Spurning an invitation to join his father's manufacturing business in Dorset, he went to Canada for five years 'doing all sorts of jobs a young man on an adventure would do – driving a truck, working on timber areas, in factories, gardens and farms.' His initial success as a businessman came in Nigeria, where he became involved in exporting and importing.

> As you can imagine, for a young man in his twenties, the whole idea of the west coast of Africa was an enormous thrill. I had an awareness of what was available in Europe and on arrival in Lagos I visited various importing companies, met people, introduced myself and tried to find out what they needed. Having gathered a shopping list of their requirements I returned to Europe and went about securing various agencies to represent manufacturers and suppliers for the sort of goods that were needed.

In fact, he became the definitive middle man and that led him, almost inevitably, to the Middle East where he became immersed in the oil and energy business. It was during this period that de Savary is believed to have built up his fortune, which later enabled him to buy into other significant business interests, although he has always seemed rather reticent about precisely how he achieved the status of a tycoon. He eventually bought a major stake in LandLeisure, at the time a barely profitable Midlands property group, which he quickly turned into a company capitalised at over £125m. In a twelve-month period LandLeisure's market value rocketed by no less than two thousand per cent after three rights issues and nine acquisitions together valued at around £100m. They included a hotel in Folkestone, property development along the M4 corridor, and an exclusive West End gaming club, formerly owned by John Aspinall.

LandLeisure was later sold to another leisure group for £180m, but de Savary retained his interests in Land's End and the Falmouth marina project.

Getting a foothold in the leisure industry was a major part of de Savary's overall strategy.

> I take the entrepreneurial view that over the next few years people are going to have more and more leisure time and they are going to learn to use their leisure time much more effectively. People will want to do more things with their leisure time so there will be a lot more opportunities to cater

> for that. Generally speaking, in this country, the provision of leisure-time activities is of a rather low grade unlike in America where they cater for people's leisure time fantastically well. I think we are a long way behind in this country. Part of the problem is that the average English businessman doesn't understand how – and considers it almost *infra dig* – to serve people, and leisure is about serving people. You're in a service business. You've got to be nice to people; you've got to consider their needs; and you've got to give them value for money. Traditionally in England we don't do that very well. You see it in the quality of waiters. To be a waiter in France is almost a craft. In England if you're a waiter, it's almost best to keep it quiet.

Highland Participants, the oil and gas investment vehicle, in which de Savary has a major stake and which acquired the Falmouth Ship Repair Company from the A and P Appledore Shipyard Management Group, was badly in need of de Savary's magic touch. It was making losses when de Savary became the majority shareholder.

But it was not de Savary's business activities that earned him a high profile in the first instance. His flamboyant life style and flair for publicity have frequently made him headline news in recent years. Before 1980 he was simply known as a shy Bahamas-based banker who'd made his money in Africa and the Middle East. Then he launched a challenge for the prestigious America's Cup. It took him two years and £6m to mount the British Challenge in 1983 – and it failed. But in the attempt de Savary became a household name and he seemed to relish the public attention. Andrew Spedding, team manager of Britain's 1983 America's Cup challenge at Rhode Island in the US, sums up the quality that has probably served de Savary best in both his business and sporting achievements: 'He's a consummate salesman. He's the sort of chap who'd sell used plutonium to Greenpeace and make them believe it was wheat.'

Spedding does not believe that de Savary will give up easily in his attempt to put Falmouth on the world map. De Savary himself sees it as the place where his sporting and business ambitions can combine in one magnificent achievement.

> When we win the America's Cup – and I mean when – and defend it in Falmouth, then of course you get a once in a lifetime chance to establish yourself economically with an enormous bonus, because during the period of the defence you really have available to you every type of support in terms of infrastructure and available capital for investment. What you must do is make good use of that so that when the America's Cup has been and gone you've actually set up your local environment to survive on its own. That's what happened in Newport, Rhode Island. It's happened in Perth and should the cup come to Falmouth, that's what will happen there too.

All the investment de Savary is pouring into Cornwall has come at a critical time. In November 1987 an urgent conference, chaired by Prince Charles, was held in Newquay to try to come to grips with what one expert has described as 'a terminal decline' in Cornwall's economy. Unemployment in the region is well above the national average. In such grim times de Savary is being hailed as a saviour and the injection of his millions welcomed like a life-belt thrown to a drowning man. De Savary is concerned that expectations of the contribution he can make might be too high, but he does accept that there should be a philanthropic aspect to an entrepreneur's ambitions.

> The challenge of one's life is to be creative and part of that – and I stress only part – is reflected in financial terms. There are many other ways to measure one's success. Certainly, I do some things that have no financial basis to them at all. I do them because I like to do them. They interest me and enthuse me or because I feel sympathetic to a particular cause or group of people. Money is not important to me. I intend to have given it all away if I haven't spent it by the time I die. I do not wish to die leaving a power mountain of money for anybody. I don't think that people inheriting fortunes from their parents or grandparents is particularly healthy. I think everyone should do his own thing and be creative in his own right.

De Savary cites his planned £35m development of the Falmouth waterfront as an example of where money takes second place to pride in a worthwhile achievement.

> I want to create something there that will truly be an example to others all over the country as to what you should do when you create a brand-new development. For that reason, I shall spend £5m more than I need to. If you like, I am reducing my profit by £5m in order to have something which I think will be magnificent. I would rather sacrifice £5m to create something that will be acclaimed and will be part of Falmouth for the next five hundred years.

Once de Savary has decided to go ahead with a new project he rarely wastes much time in getting things moving. When he took over the Falmouth Docks, for example, it was losing around £100,000 a month. A few months later it was making that amount. Similarly, his plans for improving the facilities at Land's End had been drawn up within weeks of taking over. They included restoring an eighty-bedroomed hotel that had been closed for ten years and the creation of an audio-visual enactment of the evolution of Cornwall's rugged coastline over the past 100,000 years. He also swiftly set about solving the severe erosion problem at Land's End. For a hundred years experts had declared there was nothing that could be done to repair the damage from the hordes of trampling feet. De Savary claims to have solved the problem within ninety days.

> I'm certainly not an expert on erosion, but I have been around the world and I know a lot of people. I take the view that if the problems of the space shuttle can be solved, nobody should tell me we can't deal with a bit of bloody erosion. There's always somebody somewhere in the world who can solve it if you just take the trouble to look for him.

But de Savary is careful to balance entrepreneurial risk with secure investments. Fortunately, many of his other business interests are solidly asset-backed in property and exclusive clubs.

> I like to see a spread between things that are strong in assets, things that have good earnings and things that are

> geographically well spread – even to the extent of being international rather than just in this country – and things that are in totally different market sectors. So if we go through a period of time where the hotel industry is in decline and suffering, perhaps the harbour management business in far-off countries is booming or vice versa. We never expect all our business interests to be in bonanza years at the same time. Everything has its cycle – aviation, shipping, everything – and what we try to do is to have a sufficient spread of interests so that, regardless of those cycles, the overall result of our activities is on an ever-increasing performance.

De Savary has even managed to make a business success of his own home – Littlecote, a seventy-two roomed, thirteenth-century mansion in the Berkshire countryside at Hungerford. He covers the upkeep by opening its doors to a quarter of a million visitors each summer. He was shrewd enough to sell the mansion's collection of armour for £500,000 to the Royal Armouries while at the same time managing to keep it displayed at Littlecote.

Typical of his fast-moving style is the way he sold for £50m the international chain of St James's clubs which he built up with meticulous attention to opulence, and then promptly spent £90m acquiring Aspinall's, the exclusive Curzon Street club in London (which he later disposed of with the sale of LandLeisure). He argues that he had squeezed all the development potential he could out of the St James's clubs, but that Aspinall's represented a unique property-development opportunity as well as being 'a huge cash generator' on the gaming side.

> It's a major piece of real estate with roads on three sides. Very little of the property is used for the gaming business. Part of the property is not used for anything. I am only interested in creative management. I want to take a box of matches worth £1 and turn it into £5. Once I've done that there's no point in hanging on to it for another five or ten years just to see its value increasing at the rate of inflation. I'm not a caretaker. Once the potential of a business has been developed and realised and it then moves into the area of caretaking and maintaining, it is less stimulating for me personally.

De Savary badly wants to be taken seriously as a pioneering businessman. He has been trying to live down the image of a playboy, which he claims is totally unjustified. This perception of him has been fuelled by fancy-dress parties at Littlecote, attended by royalty and society belles, coupled with his penchant for gambling clubs. He insists that basically he is very anti-social.

> I'm not a party-goer and, contrary to popular belief, I've never been a playboy. I decline ninety-nine per cent of the invitations that are extended to me. I work six, sometimes seven, days a week; start at seven in the morning and finish anywhere between eleven and midnight.

A lot of his time is spent sifting through the hundreds of proposals that are sent to him seeking his patronage. He rejects far more than he backs. But just looking them over leaves him little time for leisure activities, although he does derive pleasure from owning a fine collection of vintage cars.

He refutes any suggestion that owning a seventy-two roomed house, could in any way be regarded as ostentatious living.

> I think it would be hard for anybody to say that. Somebody has to live in the house. If nobody lives there, it will fall into disrepair and it's one of the most precious properties in England. The bulk of it was built in the 1200s and the rest in the 1500s and it's a very fine country house. It's part of our heritage and part of what makes England a magic place to live. I think people who live in these kind of houses and take the trouble to invest money in them are worthy people. I choose to do it by opening it to the public and letting the public share the pleasure. I love seeing on a Sunday eight thousand people walking around it having a marvellous time. I find that very stimulating.

Although he denies living ostentatiously, de Savary does admit that one of the benefits of being a successful entrepreneur is that he lives comfortably.

> Every man will have his own idea of what 'comfortably' means. I am not a wasteful person. I may on occasions be

extravagant, but that's a conscious decision. I cannot stand waste of any kind. I've never inherited anything and I know what it's like to have a wife and child and wonder where you're going to get the money to pay the rent or buy the groceries for the weekend. When you've been through that experience you're rarely wasteful. You may occasionally buy a beautiful painting which others may call extravagant, but to you that's an investment and a very lovely thing. Being successful allows you to enjoy some of the lovely things in life. I live in a very nice house; there are some very beautiful things in it.

A self-made millionaire, de Savary has some profound advice for young ambitious entrepreneurs who would like to follow in his footsteps. He believes that travelling the world and getting a broad experience of international affairs, as he did in his younger days, is invaluable.

But before you do that, you have to come to terms with yourself on certain fundamental principles which you have to believe in and live by during your career. Otherwise the experience you may gain from seeing the world and travelling and doing whatever you might do will be somewhat wasted.

I think you have to first learn to be honest with yourself. In other words, never believe your own bullshit. It's easy to convince yourself of anything, but if you've made a mistake, if something has gone wrong, face up to it and do the best you can to correct it. Never be afraid to say; I've screwed up. The quicker you realise that, take remedial action, damage control, the better it will be. It sounds simple, but it's quite a hard thing for a lot of people to cope with, because it inevitably means others will know – whether it's telling your partner, your bank manager, the press or your shareholders. It's easier said than done to look them in the eye and say you made a mistake. An entrepreneur must have that ability. He must be just as fast at recognising and owning up to an error of judgement as he is at seizing an opportunity.

Secondly, if one wants to be truly successful, you have to face the fact that nothing is easy in life, unless you have an undue degree of good luck. There are no short cuts to hard work. You have to work very hard. The other thing I think you have to remember at the end of the day is that there is no substitute for kindness. You can be tough; you can be hard, be ruthless; you can be all of these things. But if you lack the streak of kindness you will probably be unhappy and your victories in life will be rather hollow. You may end up a very lonely person. I have seen many examples of that – people who have made enormous fortunes, but ended up extremely lonely. I could give you a list as long as you like. The reason you need that streak of kindness is that as you go through your life you will deal with people who may seem to be insignificant at the time and who may not be all that powerful. But you never know when in life you will meet them again – and when you meet them again the lieutenant may have become a brigadier-general. The man who was opening and closing the factory gate may have become the chairman and captain of industry. The way you treat other people is probably the way they're going to treat you and therefore it's very important just to behave in a kindly, courteous, polite, considerate, gentlemanly fashion.

It doesn't stop you being hard or tough at all, but it's a balance between those two things, because we all need help; we all need favours; we all need contacts, introductions; we all need a hand. There's nobody too big who doesn't need help at some time and you need to build those things up through your life. You can't wake up aged fifty and suddenly say: I'm now going to decide to have a lot of friends. It doesn't work like that. You have to build them up over a lifetime from the age of eighteen, and when you become forty or so, as I am, hopefully you find you have a great number of people who just like you and you can pick up the telephone and say: Charlie, what do you know about this? And Charlie will tell you the truth. He'll be honest with you and I think that's one of the greatest assets an entrepreneur should have. He should have enormous loyalty himself to people and he should have due to him great loyalty from others. My telephone always rings because whether or not I take on a project people know I will treat them fairly and squarely. I won't steal their idea. I won't cut them out. I'll be loyal to them.

Sir Adam Thomson

Born: Glasgow, 1926.
Educated: Rutherglen Academy; Coatbridge College; the Royal Technical College, Glasgow.

Sir Adam Thompson was chairman and chief executive of British Caledonian Airways, the airline he founded, until it was absorbed by British Airways in 1988.

After serving as a Fleet Air Arm pilot in World War II, he became a civil airline pilot, flying with British European Airways, West African Airways Corporation and later with Britavia.

In 1961, together with a small group of friends, he achieved his ambition of operating his own airline with the formation of Caledonian Airways. By the late 1960s, this had developed into Britain's largest charter airline. Nine years after its formation Caledonian Airways took over British United Airways to form British Caledonian Airways. BCal was eventually to develop into one of the world's leading independent airlines offering scheduled services. It became a significant 'second-force' airline competing successfully for many years with the major state-owned companies. BCal's route network spanned North, West and Central Africa, North America, the Middle and Far East, Europe and the UK.

After British Airway's successful bid to take over BCal, Thomson left the company and formed his own consultancy group, Gold Stag Ltd, based at Gatwick Airport.

He was awarded the CBE in 1976 and was knighted in the 1983 New Year's Honours List. He was named 'Businessman of the Year' in 1971 and has received honorary degrees in law from Glasgow University, the University of Sussex and the University of Strathclyde.

He is a board member of MEPC plc and the Royal Bank of

Scotland Group and is deputy chairman of Martin Currie Pacific Trust plc.

In March 1962, a year after Caledonian Airways had been established as a modest charter operation, its only plane, a DC-7C crashed at Douala in the Cameroons, West Africa, killing all on board, including the airline's flight operations director and the chief pilot. It was the sort of disaster from which most businesses would have found it virtually impossible to recover. But accident investigators discovered indisputable evidence that it was an inherent design fault that caused the crash and that it was no reflection on the airline's first-class crew. With dogged determination, Caledonian Airways picked itself up from the catastrophe and built up an organisation that was to become a significant second force in the airline business, competing for many years against such state-owned giants as BOAC and BEA and ultimately British Airways, when these two were merged.

BCal's success in sustaining an independent airline for so long, despite being constantly buffeted by government regulations that swung backwards and forwards like an agitated pendulum, was largely due to the emphasis it always placed on keeping the customer happy, a necessity in any service industry, but of paramount importance in the airline business. When BCal was first set up, charter airlines had a far from enviable reputation for being third-rate and unsafe compared with the established airlines operating scheduled services. Sir Adam Thomson, BCal's founder and chairman until it was sold to British Airways in 1988, was determined that his airline would provide the highest standards both in terms of the service it gave and the reliability of the aircraft it flew.

When Caledonian Airways took over British United Airways in November 1970 and started to operate scheduled routes, Thomson set out to become the airline that provided the best personal service in the world, something he and his staff strove continuously to live up to. It meant ensuring that the aircraft provided comfort, good food and that on the ground the check-in facilities were of the highest order. But Thomson placed the greatest emphasis on the attitude of his staff towards the passengers they served. He realised that this was a crucial area for winning over customers. The friendly smile, the eagerness to deal with problems could make the difference between success and failure. BCal might not have had the huge resources and the facilities of the giant state-owned airlines, but politeness and a desire to serve was a common commodity available to all.

Thomson cites the experience of one particular VIP travelling on BCal to illustrate how vital this extra attention can be. The top official was flying to Edinburgh with BCal and found that the details of his ticket did not quite match up with what was displayed on the flight departure board. He was staring somewhat perplexed at his ticket when a passing BCal air stewardess noticed his bewilderment. She immediately approached him and asked if she could be of help and was able to clear up the discrepancy, even though as an air hostess it was not actually her responsibility. Any traveller who experiences such initiative is likely to be a passenger for life.

Even when things go badly wrong on a flight, as they inevitably will from time to time because of the fickle nature of running an airline, the right attitude can impress a customer. With an aircraft either taking off or landing every twenty seconds at Gatwick at the peak of the summer, for example, congestion can often cause tiresome delays. BCal's staff always went to enormous lengths to win back a customer who, due to unavoidable circumstances, had not experienced the kind of service he or she expected.

According to Thomson, BCal had for a long time a much better reputation than British Airways for customer service, but more recently the bigger airline had started to catch up. One reason for this was that BA put most of its employees through a special course on how to keep customers happy which was run by a Swedish consulting group. BCal later put its 6,500 staff through the same programme. Notes Thomson:

> Many of the things the Scandinavians preached we had been doing anyway, but they've taken it just a stage further. One of the things we asked them to emphasise was the importance of communicating not just to the customer but to each other. They have a lot of demonstrations on how you should speak to colleagues and associates. The point they're making is the more you meld together and

> the more you communicate with each other – if you're the boss, the more you pat somebody on the head and say that was a good job – the greater the enthusiasm you are likely to develop among the staff, and therefore the more they are going to project themselves when they come in front of the customer.

One way to ensure that a high standard of customer service is achieved is to recruit the best passenger service staff. BCal established over the years stringent criteria for its selection procedures and created an interviewing team that became increasingly refined in its techniques. It was never short of job applicants, but on average only about one out of a hundred was accepted. In addition to a good education, applicants were required to be proficient in languages and have appropriate skills in other fields like nursing.

> We were looking for a combination of these things. If we got a nurse who had a fair academic background and she spoke languages, she was going to get an interview, that's for sure. We also looked for people who could stand up to flying all night. They had to have the right disposition so that they didn't get shirty or aggressive even if they were unfairly challenged. In other words, they needed to be somebody who can keep their cool. One unsatisfactory stewardess can upset a whole cabin.

BCal did not rely purely on its own observations to convince itself that its services were amongst the highest of any international airline. It always made a practice of circulating questionnaires amongst its passengers and it received a large number of letters both complaining about, and complimenting it on, its services. The comments were broken down into various categories covering food, cabin facilities and check-in service, for example. Travelling by plane is a stressful experience for a lot of people and when things do go wrong many of them tend to get extremely worked up, and writing a letter to the airline concerned is a good way to get it out of the system. However emotional a letter seemed to be, BCal took great pains to investigate the complaint and to give a detailed reply. It treated every complaint seriously.

> Every customer was terribly important to us and we found over the years that if we received a letter describing a situation where we did make an absolute mess of something which was likely to result in the loss of that customer, it was best to answer the complaint right away. We took the trouble to answer the actual points raised, to apologise right away and maybe send a bunch of flowers. I'm sure we got ninety per cent of them back simply from writing the right kind of letter. It wasn't bull either. We really did want to give them a better service than somebody else.

As chairman, Thomson responded personally to all the letters specifically addressed to him.

Another way Thomson used to check whether BCal's service was up to scratch was to fly over the airline's route network himself. His official duties as chairman took him quite frequently to the United States and other areas of the world the airline served. Sceptics would of course say that a cabin crew is likely to be on its best behaviour when it knows that its top man is on board, but Thomson claims that it is a fallacy that a cabin crew can operate to unnaturally high standards for the length of time most long-haul flights take.

> I doubt if they can fake the service for even three hours. They'll lapse very quickly into their normal pattern of operation. There's no way they can fake it for any length of time, so you can get a good feel for it. Even if they are trying that little bit harder, it's only a small increment on top. If the service goes down it goes down for everybody.

Sir Colin Marshall, the dynamic chief executive of BA, is reported to have in his office a VDU that alerts him whenever a BA aircraft takes off or lands five minutes late in any part of the world, however remote. Thomson never took his concern for a reliable service to such technical extremes. But BCal, under Thomson, did have regular weekly briefing meetings at which performance and punctuality were two of the main issues discussed. All unusual occurrences up to the previous Sunday night were brought to the attention of the airline's top directors at the Monday morning meetings. The director responsible for the area in which the deviation occurred was then required to report back to the next meeting on the reasons for the aberration and what steps had been taken to rectify the problem. If, for example, it was something on the ground that caused a flight to be delayed, the director responsible for all the airline's facilities at Gatwick airport was given the task to look into the matter.

After demonstrating for more than two decades that an independent 'second-force' airline can compete against bigger, state-backed airlines and provide an equally good, if not better, service, Thomson started to have second thoughts in 1987. He reluctantly concluded that changes in the way modern airline competition was evolving meant BCal could no longer stand alone. The company had become too big to be a small specialist airline, yet was too small to compete comprehensively with the mega-carriers. Having extolled the virtues of competition and independence for so many years, he found himself declaring uncharacteristically to the press that big was now beautiful, and that the way forward for BCal was to join forces with another major airline so that their combined resources could take on the might of the major US and Far Eastern airlines.

Thomson maintains that the change of heart was unavoidable. He entered into discussions with several leading international airlines. This triggered an approach from BA suggesting that the two British airlines should merge. A £237m deal was announced and Thomson and Lord King, who had for so long been rivals, found themselves in the unaccustomed position of being on the same side of the fence. But opponents of the proposed merger persuaded the Office of Fair Trading to refer the issue to the Mergers and Monopolies Commission and Thomson had to wait patiently for several months for the outcome.

In the meantime the Stock Market crash in the autumn of 1987 brought about a dramatic slump in share prices and when the green light was given for the merger to go ahead Lord King returned to the negotiating table with a considerably reduced offer price. This caused Thomson to give serious consideration to a rival offer from the Swedish airline SAS. But eventually BA upped its figure to the point where Thomson had little option but to recommend it to his shareholders. BCal was finally swallowed up by its former arch rival.

Thomson insists that the merger does not represent a complete about-face of his long-held views about the desirability of competition in the airline business.

It's not a step away from competition. It's a recognition of the new type of competition that is evolving at this particular moment. We've already seen this in the US with the deregulation programme there. I suppose there are about seven airlines left there now and most people in the air transport industry feel we shall probably end up with five big airlines there and that the others will all disappear. This will be as much as anything because of the sophisticated computer reservation systems that are available today and the development of hub-and-spoke networks. The whole idea now is that rather than people flying from all sorts of different points to make their connections with long-haul flights, places like Atlanta, Chicago, Dallas and Los Angeles will be developed as hubs which will be fed along specific spokes by the local airlines.

That brings in a lot of sophisticated electronic gear, because what the airlines want to do of course is maximise the return they get on the aeroplane. There's only one way you can really control this and that is with a thundering great computer and that's why big is beautiful these days. The people who actually control the computers direct the traffic in a way that ensures they get the maximum yield out of the aeroplane for every flight. It's very difficult to do that on a smaller scale.

BCal found it increasingly difficult to get connecting flights out of the States because every airport you go to you find a mega-carrier. The bigger you are the more services you have into the US and the better chance there is of getting into somebody's computer network on a fairer basis and, in addition to that, a better chance of being able to sell yourself into the feeder areas. There are lots of BA and BCal offices scattered around the US, which, combined, give you more strength, and the rest of the air transport industry recognises that big is necessary and beautiful. You've got to be big and beautiful to survive. The bigger European airlines, like BA, Air France, Lufthansa and possibly Alitalia are the ones that are going to have the strength really to develop this type of hub-and-spoke network in Europe.

Thomson admits it came hard for him to have to surrender the airline's independence, having built it up from such humble beginnings.

> The airline as we know it today was formed in 1971 from the Edwards Committee Report that recommended there should be two major British airlines. BEA and BOAC were still around then, so in fact it would be three, but essentially two because they were going to merge. The recommendation was that a private-sector airline should become a measuring stick and a competitor to the new BA that was about to be formed. Routes were to be transferred to BCal to allow it to rise to a certain level. At the end of the day it was a great big fudge, compromises all over the place, and instead of becoming the size that we should have done under the Edwards recommendations we were held down to a smaller size at that particular time.

BCal managed to cope with this less than satisfactory situation and was holding its own when the Labour Government came to power and Peter Shore, the minister responsible, decided BCal should operate in Africa and South America, but nowhere else outside Europe. This meant that BCal's future was precariously linked to two unstable continents. When the Falklands war broke out, Thomson's worst fears were confirmed. The airline was unable to operate a large part of its network in South America. Some eighteen months later government policy changed again and BCal was permitted to develop some long-haul routes to the US and the Far East.

By 1983 things were looking up again for BCal. The government reviewed airline policy as a consequence of plans for BA to go public. The Civil Aviation Authority was asked by Nicholas Ridley to review the structure of the industry against the background of the privatisation of BA. The CAA recommended a large number of route transfers from BA to BCal to make the latter a true competitor. But history repeated itself: the original plans were watered down. Even the minor advantages

BCal was likely to get out of the plan were squashed in cabinet. 'In spite of all our efforts to develop in these different parts of the world, we were always at the point where we were just a little bit too small.'

The lesson to be drawn from such developments is that those who are in the forefront of the volatile airline business cannot afford to be rigid in their approach and must have the flexibility to change with the times, even when it means reversing some of their most fondly held beliefs. Experience constantly taught Thomson of the necessity for such flexibility ever since the 1960s when he first struggled to move from a purely charter operation to scheduled services.

> We tried for scheduled services under the old Air Transport Licensing Board on three different occasions and were frozen out each time by BEA and BOAC, but during the 1970s and the early 1980s we gradually pulled away from the charter market and became a pure scheduled carrier, apart from the fifty per cent stake in Cal Air, which was a separate charter carrier, jointly owned with Rank.

Whatever the obstacles, Thomson never allowed himself to be deflected once he had set his heart on creating his own airline. He was a Fleet Air Arm pilot during World War II and after being demobbed in 1947 he found it very hard to get a job as a pilot, particularly as he had been flying single-engine aircraft in the navy. He and a friend resolved to create their own employment by setting up their own company. The idea was to use an old Walrus amphibian plane to fly joy rides along the British coast and above spectacular mountain scenery, taking off from Lakes. But at the last moment the financial backing they thought they had secured fell through. So Thomson, at the age of twenty-one, had to be content with flying for other airlines for several years, though he never gave up looking for ways to launch his own operation.

He decided to get some experience of piloting larger aircraft and flew for BEA for a while. He also flew out in West Africa for another airline before returning to the UK to work for a company called Britavia, part of the Silver City P&O group at the time. His main job was flying troops around the world, but as the British empire began to shrink, the demand for the service also waned. An entrepreneur at heart, Thomson was constantly on the alert for commercial opportunities and landed some valuable contracts for Britavia, even though he was only a pilot. Eventually he hit on the idea of flying passengers at cheap charter rates to North America, and holidaymakers out to East Africa to visit the game reserves. Nothing like it existed at the time and he costed it all out and drew up a proposal which he presented to his employers. Although interested in the idea, they weren't prepared to give it the go-ahead. Thomson was so convinced the idea had merit, he resolved to operate the service himself. He discussed the idea with John de la Haye, who was in the charter business working for Eagle Airways in New York at the time, and the two of them decided to go into business together. Caledonian Airways was born.

From the start, Thomson and his partner had a clear vision of where they wanted their airline to go.

> We had a grand design to develop a long-haul charter airline with the objective of gradually moving into scheduled services. We intended the long-haul charter business to concentrate on the North Atlantic, Africa and the Far East. The main opportunities were on the North Atlantic routes, but we were only allowed something like six flights a year to the US at that time. We were, however, allowed unlimited flights into Canada and that was really the time the affinity market was developing on the North Atlantic routes. So we flew a lot into Canada and a limited amount into the US.

Two years later, in 1963, Caledonian Airways employed a lawyer in Washington to get a change in the regulations of the US Civil Aeronautics Board and the airline was granted the first charter permit for unlimited flights into the US, which was signed by no less a figure than President Kennedy. That was followed by permission to fly into the US from anywhere in Europe not just the UK. One breakthrough followed another as Caledonian Airways pioneered chartered flights across the Atlantic. But it was not to be until 1969/70 that the airline was to make the major breakthrough into scheduled flights as a result of the Edwards Committee Report.

In the early days Thomson would still get into an aircraft and fly off to some remote part of the world 'at the drop of a hat'. But as the airline began to expand he realised that he would have to make up his mind either to fly aeroplanes or stay on the ground. By 1965, his responsibilities for running the airline left him in no doubt that he would have to give up flying. He realised that managing such a growing organisation could not be done by the seat of the pants. He as managing director, John de la Haye who was then chairman, and three other directors sat down and worked things out,

> in a logical managerial fashion. Some of them had more experience than I did as far as management was concerned. We had a good chief accountant and we worked very closely to our budget.
>
> About thirty airlines have gone out of business from the time we started Caledonian Airways. Most of them went under because they allowed themselves to become too obsessed by their enthusiasm for aeroplanes. We sat down and said: 'We are not just in the airline business; we are in business.' We were determined not to go the same way as the failed airlines and therefore we realised Caledonian Airways had got to be a business from start to finish. We convinced ourselves that what we had was a product and that was all it was and we were in the business of making money. We weren't just flying for the sake of flying. It sounds terribly gauche and simple, but that was basically our business philosophy.

The airline directors succeeded in following that philosophy, because all through the 1960s the airline was profitable, while at least ten other airlines went bust. They resisted the temptation to purchase gleaming new aircraft which were better than the machines they were currently operating, and lived within their means. They only acquired another aircraft when the growth of the business indicated it was the sensible thing to do. The airline graduated from DC-7Cs to Britannias, to 707s and BAC 1-11s and, after taking over British United Airways, to DC-10s and finally 747s.

Thomson made the transition from pilot to head of a major

airline with comparative ease. The area he found most difficult to master was dealing with the unions. Caledonian Airways operated throughout the 1960s with virtually no union representation, but the situation changed in the 1970s after the airline took over British United Airways which was heavily unionised.

> When we moved into the 1970s and became part of government policy as a second-force airline, one of the conditions that was imposed on us was that we should recognise the unions. That was a new ball game for me and I found it very difficult in the early 1970s when we were struggling for our existence and trying to make a go of being a second-force airline to every now and again have to consult with the unions. I did it in the end by forming a small council made up of two representatives from each union in the company. We would sit around the board-room table and I would tell them the same information as the board had. I would frankly tell them what the problems were as well as the prospects. I found it worked quite well until the feeling arose towards the end of the 1970s that these union people who were in the board room talking to us were getting too far removed from their members. Some of them decided they would stay out and they would stay away for about six months and then come back in again. Then in the early 1980s they decided they didn't want this association at all, so we wound it up.

Thomson was not altogether sorry, since he found the council meetings something of a mixed blessing. Apart from the problem of the union representatives finding it hard to retain their identity, managers within the airline felt shut out and to a certain extent that their role was being usurped. The shop stewards who weren't able to attend the meetings also resented their exclusion. However, Thomson came up with an alternative approach which proved to be highly effective. It was a scheme called 'Way Ahead', which had been pioneered at English China Clays. The Cornish company had introduced the programme at a time when it was working flat out and needed its work-force to do a lot of overtime. The ECC employees were offered higher than average rates of pay provided they gave an undertaking to finish whatever needed to be done without demanding any overtime pay. Among other things, the scheme meant there were no advantages to be gained from stringing out the work. The consultant who had successfully devised the scheme at ECC was hired by BCal to introduce a similar programme at the airline.

> It took two years to get the scheme into the hangar, which is where the biggest labour force was, but in the end we had people crossing all the lines in the hangar and they worked hard to get the job finished so they could go home. If it wasn't finished, they stayed until it was.

The scheme paid handsome dividends during the severe winter of 1987. The big freeze-up resulted in planes being stranded and many engineers were unable to get to work. When eventually things started moving again there was a heavy backlog. According to Thomson, the engineers, without any prompting from him, volunteered to keep working as long as necessary to get on top of the problem. They worked solidly for three or four days without demanding any extra money or overtime payments.

Some setbacks, however, are too severe to be solved simply by dedicated teamwork. Thomson and BCal underwent one of their gravest tests during the oil crisis of 1973/74. The airline had just started operating to New York and Los Angeles. It could hardly have been a more unfortunate time to be faced with an oil shortage and escalating fuel prices. By the summer of 1974 it had become very apparent that BCal would be unable to continue its flights to the US and that it was going to have to introduce a rationalisation programme to cope with the situation. Thomson and his board devised a survival plan, which meant curtailing flights to New York and Los Angeles and a dozen or so other major routes and resulted in 720 employees being made redundant.

The airline's top directors met with the national officers of the unions involved and informed them of what was about to happen. They were told that a series of meetings were going to be held the next morning to explain to all the staff the decisions that had been taken. Those selected for redundancy would find a letter on their desk to that effect when they returned to their stations. It was all done on a very equitable basis. Five of the airline's directors were also laid off and BCal received the full support of the unions involved for the emergency action. After that, it was a question of slowly building up a recovery programme. This was seriously hampered by the appearance on the international airline scene of Sir Freddie Laker and his revolutionary Skytrain concept. Although Laker, like Thomson, was a great advocate of free enterprise, his radical new approach had repercussions which reverberated adversely for BCal.

> The worst of it was that the airline business is a highly regulated industry and only two airlines were allowed to fly into New York. Laker had got his operation into New York and we were not allowed to fly in at that particular time. Later, under the Bermuda 2 Agreement, as it was called, we were allowed to fly in, but even then we were excluded from Los Angeles because Laker was already there. So it was a great nuisance as far as we were concerned. We were convinced that Laker couldn't survive, particularly in Los Angeles. New York is the biggest international market in the world, so you can have lots of airlines going in there, but a limited number of airlines go into Los Angeles. Laker was operating on this Skytrain basis, which was to pack them in, and that works very well in the summer in Los Angeles. Because there are so many people going back and forth there's enough for everybody, as well as being a bit left over for the charter companies.
>
> Laker actually diverted a large part of the charter business on to his own aeroplanes in the summer. Then what was to happen in winter? There are very few charter passengers from Los Angeles in winter, so that was obviously something he was going to run into problems with. Then he ordered ten airbuses in the expectation of getting twenty-five new routes in Europe. They weren't there. There was no possibility of getting these routes in Europe and these aeroplanes cost a lot of money. It clearly wasn't going to work.

During his career Thomson has been a non-executive director on the boards of a number of companies which has given him the opportunity to see how other businesses outside of airlines operate. He is left with the conviction that the airline business is one of the toughest industries to operate in, largely because 'there are so many variables involved in it'. But he has no regrets.

> If I hadn't enjoyed it, I wouldn't have done it. There's never been a dull moment and I've met people all around the world as a result of being in the airline business. I particularly like going to the United States. They are always so enthusiastic and morale is a very important factor in the airline business.

So would he recommend a top job in the airline business to ambitious young executives? 'I think it depends on the individual. If you're in this type of business it's terribly demanding. You either have to give it the time and attention that is required or you don't come into the game at all.'

Sir Francis Tombs

Born: Walsall, Staffordshire, 1924.
Educated: University of London.

Sir Francis Tombs is chairman of Rolls-Royce and played a major role in the company's privatisation programme in 1987.

He began his career with the British Electricity Authority in 1948. He became director of engineering for the South of Scotland Electricity Board, subsequently becoming deputy chairman and chairman. From 1977 to 1980 he was chairman of the Electricity Council for England and Wales. He was chairman of the Weir Group plc from 1981 to 1983. He is chairman of Turner & Newall plc and a director of Shell UK Ltd and of N.M. Rothschild & Sons Ltd.

He is also chairman of the Engineering Council, chairman of the Advisory Council for Applied Research and Development, pro-chancellor and chairman of the Council of Cranfield Institute of Technology, vice-president of Engineers for Disaster Relief and a member of the Standing Commission on Energy and the Environment. He is past chairman of the Association of British Orchestras.

It was early on in his career when he was an operations engineer at a power station while working for the electricity supply industry that Sir Francis Tombs learned one of the most important lessons about being an effective manager. The power station operated around the clock and Tombs was responsible for both the day and night shifts. But it was of course impossible to be available twenty-four hours a day, so he had to master the art of delegation. If there were any major problems while he was off duty, he would be informed about them by telephone and he had to make up his mind whether it was something he should attend to personally or delegate to somebody else.

> It was quite character forming in the sense that you had to judge at some distance away whether the guy was capable of coping with the situation or not. What I learned was that some of the guys I could rely on totally and some I couldn't trust at all. An important part of delegation is getting to know who you can totally trust. You can't just delegate uniformly. Delegation is highly variable, I find. You can trust one guy totally, another one eighty per cent, another one only twenty per cent. It was a very useful period in my career, because you came up against people with confidence in themselves and people who were scared of themselves.

As a result, delegating responsibility has never been a problem to Tombs as he has made his way to the top of the electricity supply industry and of several leading engineering firms, including the Weir Group plc, Turner & Newall, and ultimately to the chairmanship of Rolls-Royce.

> I've always worked very hard at delegation on the principle that if you can get somebody else to do all the work, you are likely to get promoted. I always find that if you make spare time, if you organise yourself out of a job, nature doesn't like that; it gets filled up. People are too protective about delegation. They think they're weakening their position. I think they're strengthening it, because if they delegate properly they're running a tight outfit and they have time to take on more responsibility. I tell young managers two basic lessons about delegation that they have to learn. The first is that the guy to whom you delegate will make mistakes you wouldn't have made yourself and that's why you are where you are and he's where he is. It's the nature of things. If you're senior, you would have done the job you've just left with more experience than the new man.
>
> The second, much more difficult thing to accept, is that the guy you delegate to will do things in a way you wouldn't have done and perhaps in better ways. That's tough

> to recognise. Whenever that has happened to me I've been delighted. I've learned from it.

Many decisions, however, are too important to delegate and Tombs has on a number of occasions in his career been left with agonising judgements to make about malfunctions in the power industry. On one occasion a young engineer closed down the wrong valve causing the water to drain out of the boiler at a power station. The wrong decision could have been disastrous.

> We really either had to close the unit down, which was the safe thing to do, or to take a chance, which was a real risk. I took a chance and it was all right. That's something from which you can only derive personal satisfaction. Nobody ever knows or recognises what you have done – unless you were wrong!

When Tombs became involved in nuclear power stations the stakes were even higher. He never took safety risks, but he was faced with a potentially catastrophic situation when he was about forty-five and was director of engineering for the South of Scotland Electricity Board. If he had made the wrong decision it could have cost millions of pounds to put right.

> We had a major problem with one of the new generation of reactors in that it was discovered that a particular type of steel we were using at the core, which was largely inaccessible, was corroding fairly rapidly and we couldn't wait several years to accumulate data. So it was necessary to make quite a major judgement – as often happens in engineering – on inadequate data. The decision I made turned out to be right. There again, it was an unsung decision. If it had gone wrong it would have been in all the headlines. Because it went right nobody gave a damn.

Making the right judgements about people is just as important as being able to sum up the gravity of technical problems, in Tombs's view. One of the most vital skills he feels he has developed over his long career is the ability to judge people more acutely and to spot trouble signs much sooner.

I make a practice of talking to people who work for me, looking at them and seeing how they react – whether they're unduly pale, whether they're tired or twitchy. I make a practice of being interested in their home life. All those things come into it a lot. I think when I was a younger manager I wouldn't have bothered with that sort of detail. It pays off because you get early signs of people under stress. If someone's got marital trouble, for example, or a child ill, it's bound to have an impact, as does alcoholism. I've picked up one or two alcoholics quite early by watching them. I make a practice of talking to the medical officers about senior people both here and abroad and ask how they are.

But managing people doesn't just mean managing employees. It also means managing public relations and politicians, something Tombs became very involved in at the time of the privatisation of Rolls-Royce. As the group's chairman he was the main architect of the privatisation process, which meant liaising with the press, City analysts and most important of all, with politicians. For the most part his dealings with the government went very smoothly. There were only two major sticking points, both of which he successfully overcame. He has a golden rule in dealing with politicians.

The important thing is not to let the politicians get themselves into a corner and don't spring a row on them. I believe if I'm going to have a real row in giving them plenty of warning and marking out the territory early on which I intend to stand firm.

Tombs also believes it is important for a top manager to understand the physical processes of the industry for which he is responsible at any given time.

The management needs to understand the processes they're managing, whether its retailing or engineering. The guy who runs Woolworths needs to know a lot about mass marketing, purchasing, fashion and presentation – things I don't need to know about. If you're going to run a firm like Rolls-Royce you need to understand a whole series of things, some of them technical problems, the risks you're taking, the processes that are available. But you also need to know the financial processes, credit facilities for example. You need to have a much broader background than just one discipline. The multi-discipline approach is virtually essential. We are not very good at it in this country. People generally acquire the other skills in a random, casual, half-hearted way. I think we ought to spend more time in properly taking a guy out of the line for a year or six months and putting him through a solid accountancy course.

The Rolls-Royce chairman has certainly practised what he preaches. He trained as an electrical engineer, initially with GEC in Birmingham during the war years, but later in his career, when he was rapidly climbing the ladder to senior management, he resolved to take a part-time degree in economics at the University of London,

because people kept talking to me in a language I couldn't understand. I feel even more strongly today that a multi-discipline approach is really necessary for good general management. I'm not a great believer in engineers doing management education as part of an engineering course, because I think for your own self-respect and your own standing you first need to achieve something in your primary field – to become proficient in your craft if you like. But if you later go straight into general management without extending that primary skill it's not very successful.

We have at Turner & Newall financial awareness courses for engineers showing them how to run budgets, how to control cash, how to do capital appraisal and to work out discounted cash flow. Such courses are fairly widespread now but they used not to be. The thing that always astonishes me is that you find a lot of engineers who one way or another acquire a knowledge of accountancy, but if you're an accountant you don't bother to acquire any knowledge of the engineering process. It's strange. I don't know why it is.

Not that Tombs holds any brief for economics as a subject of primary importance. Although he has taken the trouble to become well versed in it, he regards it with a certain amount of disdain, as might be expected of someone with an engineering background.

> Economics is a rather esoteric subject. In fact, I have very little respect for it. It's pretentious. It tries to generalise things that can't be generalised. If you look at economic text books you find all sorts of formulae with undefinable indices. They write down relationships they can't define.

Tombs is a great believer in 'visible management' as a way to encourage employees and to motivate them to achieve the highest standards.

> I think most people would say I expect a lot from those who work for me. I expect high standards. I think that, too, came from my early days in management. I used to make a guy feel that I would let him get on with it if he would do the job as well as I could do it. I'm pretty intolerant of incompetence.
>
> I have a very simple management principle which is that at every level in an organisation the guy wants the next guy up to know how well or badly he's doing his job, and that implies some understanding and knowledge of the job the man's doing. So I think if you go around the shop floor, for example, and talk to a guy about the way in which he operates the machine and what's happening to the parts and so on, and he thinks you understand what he's telling you, that's a good thing. The guy needs to believe that you understand something about what he's doing and care about how he's doing it. That's what your leadership stems from – respect – and respect stems from a belief that the senior man is competent and knows something about the processes. If they see an amateur as a boss, they have no respect and therefore leadership can't exist.

Tombs rejects the more structured approaches to achieving high standards like Management by Objectives, in which employees agree attainable targets with their boss and measure their progress against these goals.

> I don't believe in MbO at all. I believe such systems are a very complicated way of providing alibis for management. I much prefer a more freewheeling approach. I believe in maximum delegation, maximum freedom for self-satisfaction under a generalised framework. I think you get the most out of people by giving them a high degree of freedom, by trusting them, but alongside trust goes an interest in how they are performing.

Some of those who analysed the collapse of Rolls-Royce in the early 1970s attributed the disaster largely to the fact that too much freedom had been given to the engineers in Britain's flagship engineering group, and that had there been more senior management control over budgets, for example, the unthinkable would never have happened. Tombs does not accept that too much autonomy was given to the group's engineers, but that 'trust was not accompanied by financial awareness or competence. The outfit was run by engineers who cared only about engineering and that was the old-style engineering. Today's engineers – certainly in Rolls-Royce – are concerned also with financial performance.'

Tombs, like most astute captains of industry, is only too aware of the dangers of engineers and R&D men becoming obsessed with their pet projects and allowing costs to overrun to the point that they can never be recouped by sales, but in his view it is the job of general management to ensure that doesn't happen.

> We have all sorts of aphorisms and slogans in Rolls-Royce aiming at ensuring that doesn't happen. I say, for example, 'It's no use planning a seventy-fifth birthday if you're not sure you're going to live that long.' To get to the medium or long term you've got to live through the short term. So don't just worry me with your plans for 1995. What's the profit going to be next year?

Such slogans are reminiscent of the Japanese work ethic, but Rolls-Royce hasn't yet resorted to hanging banners up in the factories. It has other constant reminders of the need to achieve efficiency and make profits. The impetus since privatisation has come from the market place and City analysts.

> Privatisation has worked wonders for Rolls-Royce, because when I first joined the group, before privatisation, nobody really cared about the accuracy of forecasts. If the forecast was out, so what? Who cared? If you went over the cash limit, the government said, 'dear, dear' but it didn't really matter. What people in Rolls-Royce now realise is that analysts and the press are interested in what we say and if we are wrong they are going to play hell about it and it's sharpened up the atmosphere in Rolls-Royce enormously.

That, in Tombs's view, is the main difference between running a public and a private company.

> When running a private company a lot of the spur comes from the market place, which includes the media and analysts and investors. In the state sector, all of the spur comes from management. The customers are powerless and the owners don't give a damn. When I was in the electricity industry we reduced the manpower from 230,000 to 160,000 over five years without a single strike, not because the market required it or the competition required it or the owners pushed for it, just because the management determined to be as good as the industry in the rest of the world. We went out looking at what we thought were the best overseas utilities and based ourselves on them. You can never replace that self-starting impetus that a good manager has. You need that as well, but it's reinforced by the market place and if you get the original initiative of the market, you are more likely to get the management initiative responding.

Tombs has had a very varied career in the upper reaches of public utilities, running state-owned corporations and heading several leading private engineering firms. He claims to have experienced little difficulty in switching from one type of ownership to another, perhaps underlining the necessity for a successful captain of industry to be versatile and adaptable.

> There are different problems that need to be approached in different ways. If you are lucky enough to have had an engineering training, if I can put it that way, you become

quite versatile. You become accustomed to logical argument and analysis. You become accustomed to getting the best information you can, assembling it as carefully as you can, realising that the last ten per cent has to be judgement. That's what engineering is. The poor manager is the guy who wants enough information to lead him to an inescapable conclusion. He's a mediocre manager.

Over the past thirty years of his very varied career, Tombs has been requested to do every job he has taken on. He hasn't applied for any of them. They have included eleven directorships. He recently resigned as a director of Celltech, the biotechnology company, because he found he was taking on too much. He is sceptical of the fact that some senior businessmen manage to handle as many as forty-five non-executive directorships at the same time.

I don't know how such people find the time to read the papers involved and consider the problems. I couldn't allow myself to go to a board meeting without having thought about the subject and read the relevant papers. The only way I would take on something new would be to stop doing something else. I can't imagine any circumstances in which I would want to do that. There's a limit to the number of non-executive directorships I can cope with, but I wouldn't be so presumptuous as to suggest others are taking on too many.

Tombs believes that the role of the non-executive director on company boards, who used to be regarded as little more than a yes-man to support the chairman, is now being taken more seriously, but he still sees problems preventing non-executive directors from playing as full a part as they might.

I think a board gets the non-executive directors it wants really. If it provides plenty of information for non-executive directors, it gets good ones, but the problem is very often – it's usually the chairman who does this – there is a lot of work involved in getting the papers into a form the non-executive directors can assimilate. What a lot of boards do is put up highly complicated technical papers which the professionals in the business have time to read and understand, but the non-executive directors haven't. You've got to be prepared to synthesise the arguments in a way that allows non complication for non-executive directors. That is a translation job that requires quite a bit of work. I usually go through the important papers with the executives before a board meeting and ask them to explain any jargon.

But in Tombs's view, it is not sufficient simply to be highly professional when heading a major group. There has to be an element of entrepreneurialism as well.

You have to be prepared as a professional manager occasionally to take chances. That's what entrepreneurialism means. If you see an opening with a possibility of profit at the end of the road, are you prepared to take it? I think a lot of professional managers look down on the term 'entrepreneur' because they regard it as synonymous with chance. I don't think you can just be a professional manager. You must have flair; you must be prepared to exploit opportunities.

Tombs is not altogether convinced that the much-vaunted power of the computer has helped to improve the quality of decisions made by top managers.

One of the great problems with engineering and management is the advent of the computer which churns out numerical data that is only as good as the input. People tend to compile a whole spectrum of scenarios and a whole spectrum of variances until I say they present you with a choice ranging from zero to infinity. So you mustn't over-analyse. You've got to use sensibly what data is available and to a large extent the weight you place on various factors is intuitive.

But I think you've got to try to be as objective and logical as the data will allow – extract all the certainties from what data there is and lay off the uncertainties. Then you have to jump the remaining gap. There always is a remaining gap. That really comes down to judgement and maybe intuition. The way you jump that gap depends on the price of jumping it. You have to assess the cost of being wrong. In my more mischievous moments I say that all the decisions that reach the chairman's desk in a big organisation must be fifty-fifty or nearly so, because otherwise they would have been settled further down. So all the chairman needs is a penny!

There is a class of decisions like that which come to the top that are fifty-fifty because there are two equally balanced factions. You've got to spot those. It doesn't really matter what you decide. You just take your choice. Then there are the very important big decisions which can't be decided because they're so indefinite and so intangible at the other extreme – issues that will have an effect in six or seven years' time when you don't know what the competition will be doing, you don't know what the state of the world economy will be, what the price of oil will be and so on.

When Tombs has a major decision of that kind to grapple with he tends to solve it by what he calls 'kicking it around. I get a group of people together and just talk about it.' A good example of this was when he was chairman of the South of Scotland Electricity Board in the mid-seventies. He had to make a major decision about the future of nuclear reactors, which involved a political skirmish. Before making up his own mind he got twenty of his key people together from various departments and discussed the issue solidly for two days.

Gradually the picture became clearer and clearer – not numerically clearer, but influentially clearer. The other thing I find very important is not to rush vital decisions, because I find the subconscious works wonders. The old saying, 'sleep on it', is very effective. The mind does tend to sort things out. It makes jumps we are not consciously aware of.

Occasionally you have to make important decisions within minutes, but a lot of managers tend to think that many decisions need to be that quick and I don't think many do. More often than people realise you can take your time. I refuse to be stampeded. There's a technique where people who want an instant decision try to pressure you into making it. It's got to be done by tomorrow. My standard response is that they shouldn't be asking me now; they should have asked me yesterday or last week.

Tombs is unequivocal about the responsibility major companies should have towards the community at large.

Their principal responsibility is to employ people in a fair way. In that I include fair rates of pay, conditions of work, training, provision of sports and social facilities and helping people when they become redundant. I also believe in companies supporting charities, but they should be related to the kind of business you are in. At Rolls-Royce, for example, we support the aviation interests or a charity close to one of our major plants.

But he sees no easy solution to the problem of wholesale redundancies.

At Rolls-Royce and Turner & Newall we try to help people made redundant find new jobs, but you can't create new industries for them. Having said that, I think we are very bad at getting rid of square pegs in round holes at the senior level in this country. The Americans are much better at it. You've got to be prepared to do that, but there's got to be fairness about the way you do it.

Neither does Tombs see any alternative to the introduction of automation in industry, even if it does result in large-scale lay-offs.

It's the only thing to do if we are going to remain competitive in the world. The alternative is to continue with very high labour costs, very high production costs and development costs. You've got to be quite hard-hearted about that. The job of the manager is to keep the business going and employ as many as he can doing it. If it's not as many as it was last year, that's unfortunate. I think it's copping out and kidding yourself to go the other way, trying to avoid unpleasant decisions and avoiding hurting people, which of course redundancy does. I always think about the families of the people who are losing their jobs. It's not to be taken lightly, but the nettle has to be grasped if the outfit is going to stay competitive. We spent thirty years post-war avoiding the problem.

Tombs is convinced that automation is going to make a major impact on society and the way future generations live their lives, but like many people he finds it difficult to define exactly what the post-industrial society is supposed to mean.

I think the notion is that we are going to move out of the highly industrialised period into a service and leisure period. I don't know how that can be supported by wealth. You're always going to have to have wealth creation and I don't think the service industries are going to be able to support a high leisure economy. The manufacturing base is extremely important. Alongside that is the fact that mechanisation is going to play a bigger role and will mean that people will have to use their time differently. I think we have been singularly bad at encouraging people to use their leisure properly and I think that one of the difficulties there is that it's got mixed up with the taxation system and I suspect that a lot of the people who are said to be unemployed are in fact moonlighting. If you want your house painted you employ a guy who doesn't charge you any VAT and doesn't pay any tax. I think we've mixed up leisure with tax avoidance to a large extent.

We complain about the moonlighters, but since society has created the situation where a guy can work Monday, Tuesday and Wednesday and have Thursday and Friday off to go fishing or play golf it's not surprising he's grown to like it, is it? The fiscal system encourages that. Some people certainly badly want jobs and feel very rejected and unhappy about society. I'm not at all sure that's the majority. I think a surprising number of people quite like being unemployed and doing a moonlighting job for two or three days a week. Life has become very comfortable. The Black Economy is one of the ways of sharing the spoils but I think it's a very

> inefficient way. I don't think it will ever be avoided because of the ingenuity of individuals. You're talking about individuals not regimented systems. Individuals will always find a way of optimising the situation. That's where creativity comes from, adapting ourselves to the circumstances and making the best of them.

Tombs is also less inclined than many top industrialists to believe that the 'them and us' attitude that has prevailed in British industry for many years will ever be entirely eradicated.

> I think a lot of people like it. The notion of a totally democratic boss and worker is not what people particularly want. I think deep down a lot of people want the boss to be remote. Then they can throw bricks at him and, if he's lucky, respect him. A lot of people want things decided for them. It would be very troublesome if everybody wanted to make decisions. So I think the notion of highly democratic management is overstated. You need a flexible, well-informed, hard-working approachable management.

Tombs does, however, believe in incentive schemes and is delighted to note that ninety-seven per cent of Rolls-Royce employees hold shares in the company and that they are constantly asking him questions about the level of the share price. They also tend to show as much concern as top management when an order is lost or late in being delivered.

Reflecting on the nature of the business environment aspiring young managers are now entering, Tombs suggests that such aspirants often set their sights too high too soon. He is critical of the promotion graphs some of them draw up for themselves at a very premature stage in their careers.

> They ought to be approaching the issue from the other view entirely. They should be working like hell at their jobs, trying to demonstrate they know what they're doing and hoping to be recognised through that route and then looking for opportunities. You can't pre-destine a plan.

The Rolls-Royce chairman does not believe that the business

environment for up-and-coming young executives is any more or any less complex than it used to be.

> There are elements of complexity and there are elements of simplification. Britain used not to be a particularly powerful exporting nation, except to the tied markets of the Commonwealth. Now we are in competition with the rest of the world. Rolls-Royce exports eighty per cent of its output all over the world and I have to learn about things like trade offset. If you are selling to Turkey, for example, you've got to buy something in exchange. There are also a lot of different financing procedures. A top manager needs to know more than his own discipline. If he's an engineer he needs to know quite a bit about international finance. He's got to know about exchange rates and how to hedge for cover. If he's an accountant he ought to know something about the processes, if it's an engineering company – what computer-aided design can do for you, for example. If he's in manufacturing what new raw materials are around, what developments are likely to change the market. If he doesn't do that he can't be in top management.
>
> A top manager also needs to travel extensively to see the overseas operations, to keep in touch with the markets and the politics, which can be quite important these days. When I go to Africa, I usually meet politicians to try and get a feel about the likely developments in that particular country. I regularly visit the Turner & Newall plants in Africa and I always go to the mines in Zimbabwe because the staff there are very isolated and it's very easy for them to feel forgotten.

Despite such an active life, Tombs has successfully avoided becoming a workaholic. His main form of relaxation is going to the opera and he spends a lot of time attending concerts of classical music and listening to compact discs of his favourite composers. Wagner is not one of them. 'I find him too pompous and tedious. I occasionally annoy my Wagnerian friends by saying what we need is a Reader's Digest version of Wagner – a forty-minute Ring! I prefer Richard Strauss. I think he's like Mozart - very intimate, not at all pompous.' Until recently he was chairman of the Association of British Orchestras, a duty he had to give up due to pressure of work.

Golf and gardening are two other leisure-time pursuits that help to take his mind off the rigours of being a captain of industry. The gardening is done at his country home in Warwickshire. He also has a flat on a golf course in France. He used to sail but has given that up mainly at the instigation of his wife. He nowadays contents himself with less rigorous activities, such as cycling from his country home to the local pub, a journey of about three or four miles. 'It's lonely and quiet. The pace is different.'

He looks upon all these pastimes more in terms of a change of pace than as an escape from work, which he clearly relishes but does not allow to dominate his life.

> I think life would be very dull if one was totally consumed by work. I'm usually away from the office by six. It's very rare it's later than that. I'm usually in before nine and I work a full day. I travel a lot but I don't believe in working weekends if I can help it. If, as is occasionally the case, I have to travel over two or three weekends in a row, I take a few days off when I get back.

Sir Graham Wilkins

Born: Mudford, Somerset, 1924.
Educated: Yeovil School; University College, South West of England (now Exeter University).

Sir Graham Wilkins is chairman of Thorn EMI plc. He was appointed chairman and chief executive in July 1985 and relinquished the chief executive role two years later. Prior to that he had been non-executive deputy chairman of the company since 1984, having joined the board as a non-executive director in 1978.

He is honorary president of Beecham Group plc, having retired at sixty as chairman and chief executive of the company in July 1984. He joined Beecham in 1945 and served in various executive positions in the consumer products and ethical pharmaceutical sectors of the business prior to becoming executive vice-chairman in 1974 and chairman in 1975. He is also a non-executive director of Rowntree plc.

He is president of the Advertising Association of Great Britain and chairman of ICC United Kingdom. He is also chairman of the review body on Doctors' and Dentists' Remuneration.

He is chairman of the Council of the School of Pharmacy and has held office as vice-president of the Proprietary Association of Great Britain, president of the Association of British Pharmaceutical Industry, chairman of the Medico-Pharmaceutical Forum, president of the European Federation of Pharmaceutical Industries' Associations and a member of the British Overseas Trade Board.

He was knighted in the Birthday Honours List in 1980, and in 1984 was voted one of the Businessmen of the Year by the Institute of Directors.

One thing that has been evident all through my business

> career is that I have always been able to get people to want to work for me. I've never believed you should necessarily tell people what you want them to do. You must make certain they do what you want, but preferably by persuading them that it was their idea. Then you're ahead of the game. Without wanting to exaggerate I have always had a facility for getting on with people and being able to get them not only to work for me, but to enjoy working for me. It's either something you've got or you haven't. I suppose I first became aware of it in my school days. If you're head boy of your school and captain of the cricket and rugby teams you gain experience of handling people, even if you don't recognise it was leadership at the time.

As chairman of Thorn EMI, one of Britain's leading companies in the 'Electricals' sector, Sir Graham Wilkins can count himself fortunate to possess such an easy facility with people. The gift was first put to the test, however, at a much earlier stage in his career. He had studied chemistry and mathematics at the University College of the South West, later to become Exeter University, and broke with family tradition by working in industry as a research chemist at the Anglo Iranian Oil Co, rather than becoming a teacher as his father had been before him. He was involved in research into fuel oil as part of the war effort at AIO, which was later to become BP. But he soon discovered that the then closeted world of the laboratory scientist was not for him.

> I don't think I could claim to have been one of the best research scientists in the world. I was probably average to good. But I reckoned I was better at managing people than molecules and so I decided that my future did not lie at a bench as a research scientist.

His decision to switch from back-room research worker to front-line manager and become more involved with people was hastened by an offer to go out to India and manage the building, equipping and start-up of a new factory for his then employers Macleans, part of the Beecham Group. The manager who had originally been assigned the task had suffered a breakdown and returned home. It was an enormous challenge for someone who had never had any formal management training, but Wilkins rose to the occasion with great confidence, already conscious of his ability to persuade others to do his bidding. He had around 150 employees under his control and carried out his task sufficiently well to be invited to stay on the manufacturing side when he returned to the UK some ten months later. He had insisted that his stay in India should be short, because he had just married and in those days it was not customary to take wives abroad on business tours of duty.

This was part of a long association with the Beecham Group. After gaining experience of manufacturing in the UK, he was posted in 1955 to Canada to become technical director of a company there that controlled all Beecham's activities in North and South America. While there he came to realise that he quite enjoyed marketing and general administration, so he eventually took over complete responsibility for that in Latin America. He admits that he did not enjoy his stay in Canada too much, because he was based in Toronto which was still only a modest-sized city then, and he found it a stark contrast to the more refined pleasures of living in London. It was an entirely different situation, however, when he moved to New York to take up total management responsibilities for the whole of Latin America.

He returned to the UK in 1959 to become assistant managing director of Beecham's ethical pharmaceutical business, which at that time was only at an embryonic stage, with sales of less than £500,000. Wilkins took charge of the division's activities worldwide after two years and was largely responsible for building it up into the major industry that it later became. He ultimately became chairman of the Beecham Group, a post he held for nearly ten years. He retired before normal retirement age at sixty, which he had always promised he would, to concentrate on outside business interests. He anticipated that these would keep him occupied for around two or three days a week. They included non-executive directorships of Courtaulds, Hill Samuel and Thorn EMI. When Sir Richard Cave retired as chairman of Thorn EMI and Peter Laister was appointed to replace him, Wilkins became non-executive deputy-chairman to provide Laister with the benefit of access to wider experience. After about fifteen months the board concluded that Laister was not the man for the job and that Thorn EMI's future viability was threatened. The non-executive directors on the board took the unusual step of firing the chairman and Wilkins was asked to take over the helm.

Colin Southgate had only recently been appointed as managing director and Wilkins told the board that he would only take on the job if he could be chief executive as well, a role he has since relinquished as a result of the company's position becoming more stabilised. 'I knew what the problems were,' says Wilkins simply to explain why he originally demanded the double role for a period.

For non-executive directors to have been so instrumental in forcing the departure of a chairman of such a leading company was something of a rare occurrence. The traumatic move may have been responsible for setting in motion a more widespread reappraisal of the role of the non-executive director in British industry. There followed similar upheavals at several other major British companies and the role that non-executive directors ought to play in corporate affairs started to be viewed in a new light – not before time in many people's minds. It was felt in many quarters that too many non-executive directors had been appointed in the past simply as supporters of the chairman. The appointments were sometimes sealed over a glass of port in the chairman's favourite club in an atmosphere of cordiality and back-scratching co-operation. As a consequence, many companies had on their boards non-executive directors who saw it as their role to support slavishly the actions of the chairman rather than to question his wisdom whenever the need arose. It was even suggested that Rolls-Royce might have avoided its collapse in the early 1970s if there had been non-executive directors on its board who had taken sterner control when the company's affairs were clearly getting out of hand.

The new attitude towards the role of the non-executive director could result in a healthier business climate in the UK, in the opinion of many observers. Wilkins is quite categorical about the issue.

> I have always seen the role of the non-executive director as one that offers advice and brings a broader outlook to a company, but the prime role of the non-executive director

is to fire the chairman when he's not doing his job. The important change that has come about is that non-executive directors are no longer solely friends of the chairman but, in addition, people who can bring a genuinely independent view and I think we at Thorn EMI helped in that movement. I am not sure if the country as a whole has woken up to it, but there is now a growing tide of opinion that says there should always be non-executive directors on public company boards and that they shouldn't just be buddies of the chairman.

Wilkins believes that a board made up of two-thirds executive directors and one-third non-executive directors is about the right balance for most companies. He does not approve of the US system where non-executive directors tend to predominate on company boards, If there are an insufficient number of executives on a board, Wilkins believes it is virtually impossible for the non-executives to learn enough about what is actually going on inside a company.

Because of the nature of its products, in recent years there had always been a fair number of scientists on the board of Beecham. For that reason, Wilkins, with his background in scientific research, never had any problem in establishing a rapport with his fellow board members during his chairmanship.

I'm not suggesting that the chairman can ever direct what areas of research scientists ought to be working in, but it does help to understand what they're talking about. I also understand some of the electronics jargon used in Thorn EMI, but the biggest part of the company's present activities is in the service sector, by which I mean our rental and retailing activities. As long as someone has demonstrated good management ability, can pick good people and can delegate, I honestly believe a senior executive in that sense would have a ninety per cent chance of running whatever industry he or she was in. But you have to have all these qualities to start with.

Wilkins's people-handling skills were put severely to the test when he took over the chairmanship of Thorn EMI and set about restoring its fortunes. 'The first task, of course, was to put some morale back into the business, because they were in dead trouble,' says Wilkins bluntly. On the first day he was appointed he and the managing director of four or five months' standing held a meeting with the top hundred executives of the company. Wilkins describes many of them as looking like 'beaten men' who were not sure where they were going, and at the time he faced a daunting task in getting the group back on an even keel. They weeded out some of the weaker managers and promoted other 'very good people' who they felt had not been given the opportunity to perform to their true potential. They also recruited in some new blood from outside the company.

> Another important aspect of management that I have been aware of from an early stage is that you have to be able to choose good people and that's not an ability everybody has. You have to be absolutely certain that once you've picked somebody you actually do give them the responsibility and make certain they undertake that responsibility. You help then in all sorts of ways – you send them on training courses, advise them and educate them – but you must be able to delegate.
>
> Getting people to work as a team is also important. When I came to Thorn EMI they weren't working as a team. There were some Thorn people and some EMI people and never the twain shall meet. We had to get rid of all that. The two companies were supposed to have merged but in fact they hadn't really. There were far too many product areas in the business and they were preoccupied with other things than maintaining and improving the profitability of the base businesses. Consequently, the businesses were going down and down. They had to be focussed. The company had to get out of quite a few areas it was in. I'm not saying they weren't interesting, but it couldn't afford to invest the sort of money that was required and some of them would never be adequately profitable.

Wilkins realised that it was necessary to make the business managers more profit-conscious. Up to then most of the responsibility for profits was controlled centrally. Wilkins quotes a graphic example of this: 'Of the £55m worth of interest the company was paying out at that time, only £5m was charged out to the operating units.' To Wilkins, making the businesses responsible for their own financial housekeeping was an elementary but essential solution. It was the sort of solution that came easily to someone trained as a mathematician and a scientist.

> I'm not saying that's a particularly good training or that it's better than anything else. After all, where higher education is concerned it's not necessarily the subjects you learn, it's developing the power to think rationally that is important. What's the situation? What's the cause? Where do we want to get to and how do we get there?

But Wilkins doesn't believe that running a company is something that should be taken totally seriously.

> I don't think anyone can really reach the top unless they've got a sense of humour. They might get to the top, but I wouldn't regard them as a fully rounded personality. I think the ability to laugh, even at yourself, is very important. I would never promote someone who in my opinion did not have a sense of humour. I'm not suggesting top managers have to be constantly telling funny stories. I suppose really it's the ability to see more than one side of a situation.

In Wilkins's view, a top executive also needs to have a broad perspective and that means keeping abreast of international markets.

> In most cases, the UK is only about five per cent of total world markets. Most manufacturing firms have to think at least pan-European. If I didn't know my opposite number in most of Thorn EMI's international competitors I wouldn't think I was doing my job properly. The two years I've been here isn't long enough to get to know them all, but I know the senior people in the top three or four Japanese companies. Certainly in my Beecham days I could call the heads of all the international competitors by their first names.

I knew them well. We would go and bang on their doors to talk to them.

Wilkins does not believe it is sufficient to obtain market intelligence about rival firms via reports. He considers it essential to find out the information first hand and that inevitably has meant a lot of travelling during his career. Flying around the world was something that used to appeal to him in his younger days, but not any more.

> After a time it simply means exchanging one office for another and having to put up with a hell of a lot of aggro in between. But you can't have a business which has any pretensions to being international unless you know what is happening around the world. You have to find out how efficient your competitors are and you have to be at least as efficient as they are. Otherwise, how can you compete?

The Thorn EMI chairman sees nothing surprising in building up a rapport with the very people he is competing against in world markets. In his Beecham days the international comradeship with the heads of rival firms meant that they would almost always pay him a courtesy call when they happened to be visiting the UK. Wilkins describes it as,

> a community of competitiveness. I don't see why I shouldn't tell my competitor something he can find out for himself if he puts a bit of effort into market research. If he can find out for himself, why shouldn't I tell him? I would expect him to tell me something in return but not giving away any future plans or anything of that sort. It happens much more easily in the US; slightly less easily in Europe; and with more difficulty in Japan.

Wilkins does not find it easy to explain what has motivated him to become a captain of industry. He has a few of the trappings associated with having made it to the top.

> I happen to live on the bank of the Thames, so obviously I've got a couple of runabouts, but you'd be hard put to it

> to grace them with the term yacht. I suppose I've always thought perhaps I was supposed to have been born rich and I wasn't, so obviously I like to have a reasonable standard of living. My parents did a very good job bringing me up with somewhat limited means and I was given as many opportunities as they could afford. But I've always believed that whatever you do you should try and do well.

Wilkins has never had any political ambitions, but he has devoted a great deal of time to trade associations, both nationally and internationally. He was formerly president of the Association of British Pharmaceutical Industry and was the founder president of the European Federation of Pharmaceutical Industries' Associations. He was also a founder member of the Medico-Pharmaceutical Forum, an association which combines in the UK the interests of the pharmaceutical industry and the medical profession. He is chairman of the British branch of the International Chamber of Commerce and chairman of the review body that makes recommendations on doctors' and dentists' salaries. He has played an active role in raising funds for the Royal College of Physicians.

In addition, he is president of the Advertising Association in the UK, a federation of trade associations representing advertisers, the media and advertising agencies. Right from his Beecham days, Wilkins has always been concerned that advertising is not properly understood by the general public and politicians and has devoted himself to trying to improve its standards and making the more positive aspects of advertising more widely known.

There is a common thread to his involvement in such a diverse range of associations.

> Beecham is probably the pre-eminent marketing company in this country and I found that many people think of marketing and advertising as being synonymous, whereas they're not. Anything I can do to disabuse people of that I will spend time doing. The International Chamber of Commerce is an organisation dedicated to pursuing free market activities around the world and I am as strong a free marketeer as you'll find anywhere. The Royal College

of Physicians and the medical/pharmaceutical associations obviously relate back to my Beecham period.

Wilkins carried out a crusade to try to get people to differentiate between marketing and advertising.

> When people talk about marketing they think of it as advertising and they forget that marketing is a fundamental business concept. There are production-orientated businesses and there are marketing-orientated businesses. In the production ones people decide what to produce and they then go out and try and sell it. In the marketing ones, they find out what people want or might want and are prepared to pay. They make the product and then go through all the sales promotion part of the activity. It goes right back to the concept of what you're going to make.

The Thorn EMI chairman admits that there is occasionally some advertising that troubles him and he is conscious that there may be a risk that some people could be persuaded into buying goods they don't really need. But that is a criticism of a particular advertisement but not of advertising itself. He questions some of the logic behind the banning of cigarette advertising.

> If the government decides to ban cigarette advertising that's something they are perfectly entitled to do. But, on the other hand, if the government allows cigarettes to be sold, why don't they then allow cigarette manufacturers at least the opportunity to explain the difference between various brands? All the evidence suggests that advertising has not actually increased the consumption of cigarettes. What it has done is polarise the particular brands.

Wilkins is equally pragmatic about another of society's serious problems – chronic unemployment.

> I feel terribly sad about the unemployment in this country and am concerned that something should be done about it. But I would be the first to say that it was absolutely right

that the overmanning in this country was sorted out. It is much better for the efficiency of this country that businesses should not be overmanned - that they should have the minimum number of people to do the job properly. Otherwise this country could never have competed internationally, unless those in employment were on very low wages. With inflation that was obviously impossible. You have to be realistic, but of course it must be awful to have to go home and tell your wife you've been made redundant.

Wilkins endorses the idea that more small businesses should be encouraged to create jobs, but he does not see that as a complete panacea.

If anybody thinks that the growth of small businesses is going to make any significant dent in unemployment in the short term they are whistling in the wind. The biggest social problem, it seems to me, is not so much the large number of unemployed, although that's serious enough in its own right. The most serious consequence to me is that children are leaving school and don't have a job and may not get one until they are in their twenties or even older than that. I honestly believe that once somebody's left school and hasn't got a job for some years, they're never going to want a job. I think they're going to become unemployable if they've gone without work for any length of time.

Wilkins is convinced that there could be another solution to the problem, although he is sometimes accused of not understanding economics when he advocates the idea.

I honestly believe that since we do have a large number of people unemployed and we have to pay them unemployment money it would be ten times better to reduce the retirement age down to fifty-five so that all the young people can get jobs. Instead of paying the young people unemployment we could use the money to pay older people early retirement pension. You wouldn't then have all these young people with idle hands making trouble.

Wilkins has been a senior executive for a large part of his business career. He was only forty when he first joined the Beecham board, so he is well placed to advise up-and-coming managers on the wisdom of striving to get to the top. Although he believes business life has become far more complex than it used to be, he does not believe that it should discourage ambitious young people from wanting to carve out a career in industry.

> I think we've somehow got to get across to younger people that there are very satisfying careers to be had in industry and that they can earn very satisfactory salaries which enable them to lead a full and complete life. It is not just the financial services sector which is the be-all and end-all of things. How you do that I don't know. I honestly believe some of the changes that have happened in industry in the last few years have been tremendous improvements. I think there is still a 'them and us' syndrome, but it's much less than it used to be and I think that's because a lot more information is being passed down the line – the more the better.

But Wilkins is not in favour of the Scandinavian notion of worker directors.

> I think calling somebody a worker director is a nonsense. What am I if I am not a worker director? Frankly, I'm not at all convinced somebody from the shop floor can make a real contribution to the direction of a major company. I suppose it could happen, but it would be a very rare event. I am more inclined to encourage things like works councils. I don't think somebody from the shop floor can really understand how a board director in that company should operate.

Summary

Before attempting to isolate the qualities common to top industrial leaders, an important distinction needs to be made. The entrepreneur who builds a business empire from scratch out of his own creative resources is a different personality from the professional manager who takes over the stewardship of an established enterprise. The entrepreneur is motivated by the sheer challenge of seeing an embryonic idea grow into a flourishing business which may in time take its place among the leading companies which together form the industrial fabric of the nation.

Once the entrepreneur feels he has extracted the maximum return from the business he has created, he will often sell it off and divert his energies to exploiting new opportunities. The professional executive, on the other hand, is absorbed by the task of maintaining the equilibrium of an established organisation which is often providing the livelihood for thousands of employees and playing a major role in the economic well-being of the country. Whereas his main aim is steady growth, the entrepreneur thrives on peaks and troughs in the business cycle. As Peter de Savary puts it:

> The entrepreneur exists out of being essentially in the right place at the right time, dealing with the right people and doing the right thing in terms of responding to opportunity very quickly, very flexibly, within the umbrella of the established companies . . . He picks up the slack or he sucks out the surplus of any given situation at any given time.

By his very nature, the entrepreneur tends to be more of a risk-taker. He usually spreads his risks by having lots of eggs in numerous baskets, whereas the career prospects of the professional manager are dependent on how well he succeeds in running the particular company of which he has charge. He brings an astute, analytical mind to the task of manipulating company resources in such a way that they will ride out whatever hazards to progress threaten business stability. It was perhaps not surprising to discover that a high proportion of the professional managers interviewed for this book shared a scientific, particularly an engineering or chemical, background.

Sir Austin Pearce, who retired in 1987 as the chairman of British Aerospace, was very conscious of the difference between the role of the entrepreneur and that of the professional manager:

> If you are running your own company which you own and have built up from scratch you have a different approach to somebody like myself who's a professional manager. That's what I am, let's face it. It doesn't matter whether I like it or not; it's a fact of life. I didn't own the companies I worked for. I've got a few shares in British Aerospace, but nobody would notice if I sold them all.

The entrepreneur tends to build a business around products and markets he feels passionately about. Good examples are Sir Terence Conran who has always been design-led in his approach to Habitat and Anita Roddick who is obsessed by the desire to persuade the world to use body lotions produced from natural ingredients. The professional top executive, on the other hand, will quite readily move from one industry to another – from coal to steel to electronics – and apply the same proven management approach regardless of what field it is in. Business leaders differ in their opinions about the extent to which it is feasible to chop and change industries, however. Sir Adrian Cadbury, for example, is very sceptical about the ability to shift from managing a bank to managing a steel mill, but Sir Monty Finniston, former chairman of British Steel, believes professional management is universally applicable.

> I don't think what you run makes any difference because I've run companies of very diverse natures and the principles that apply to British Steel at one end apply equally to a small company at the other end of the scale. What I would most strongly suggest as the conditioning factor is the people you have to work with.

Sir Adrian suggests another equally vital element. In his view 'it is essential to understand the key factors for success or failure in your type of business and I'm not convinced you can do that without actually understanding the process in some detail.' Pearce is inclined to support this view:

> I could switch from oil, which has a chemical background, to the chemical industry. I think I could go to the food industry or brewing industry. I'm an engineer by training, so I could move into something like British Aerospace. But could I switch to be chairman of Burtons, for example? That's a very different sort of activity. It's possible, but it would not be a very natural switch.

Sir Hector Laing, chairman of United Biscuits, also believes the shoemaker should stick to his last. He made his views on the subject very clear during the interview he gave for this book: 'Most of the conglomerates which were made up of a disparate collection of businesses have failed. The best businesses over a long period have been the ones with a single thrust.'

Sir John Harvey-Jones, who during his chairmanship of ICI turned a large trading loss into a billion-pound profit, insists there is a limit to the impact any professional manager can have on a major company. He dismissed the personality cult as a significant influence in business life in an interview he gave to the *Western Morning News* in November 1985.

> People think there is some sort of superman who is suddenly going to change something. The reality of life is that you have to go with the grain of your outfit. ICI has 120,000 people, so the idea that I arrive one morning and say 'turn left' and everyone turns left is not on. If you think that, you don't know many people in ICI. It's really a matter of releasing the latent energy in an organisation and heightening the abilities of people to contribute to the common gain.

The number of non-executive directorships an industrial leader can take on at any one time is also being seriously questioned. Some top men feel able to sit on an enormous number of boards.

Sir Francis Tombs, chairman of Rolls-Royce, wonders how they can possibly cope with so much responsibility.

> I don't know how such people find the time to read the papers involved and consider the problems. I couldn't allow myself to go to a board meeting without having thought about the subjects and read the relevant papers . . . There's a limit to the number of non-executive directorships I can cope with, but I wouldn't be so presumptuous to suggest others are taking on too many.

Sir Graham Wilkins, chairman of Thorn EMI, is very categorical about what the prime responsibility of the non-executive director should be, which in his view is 'to fire the chairmen when he's not doing his job.' Wilkins has observed a marked change in the role of the non-executive director in recent years. 'The important change that has come about is that non-executive directors are no longer solely friends of the chairman but, in addition, people who can bring a genuinely independent view.'

The traditional image of the ineffective non-executive director was summed up in a study by the Economist Intelligence Unit:

> They were seen as rather peripheral figures, whose presence might add lustre to the board, but contributed little, if anything, to the serious business of management. The job was regarded as a useful source of income for ex-politicians, retired civil servants and company executives who had been put out to grass.

Such patronage, although not yet extinct, seems to be very much on the wane. The more enlightened companies are now seeking non-executive directors who challenge, rather than rubber-stamp, the decisions of the board. They are looking for directors who have the courage of their convictions.

A group of leading financial institutions and employers' bodies has set up an organisation called Pro Ned, which, under the chairmanship of Sir Adrian Cadbury, promotes the wider and more effective use of non-executive directors in British industry. Douglas Strachan, who runs Pro Ned, describes its aims uncompromisingly:

> If you want to be flippant, we are here to abolish the Old Boy network, a system under which the company chairman dispenses patronage. Patronage seeks to preserve the *status quo* because it's profitable and comfortable and does not encourage constructive criticism, challenging, penetrating questioning and plain speaking which are vital attributes for a sound non-executive director. Pro Ned has done a great deal to break down the Old Boy network. People are now aware that it has a very bad name. We think it is important to take the same care over a non-executive board vacancy as it is over an executive vacancy.

This is a view supported by Sir Adrian:

> Non-executive directors of the right kind are an essential ingredient in enabling boards to operate effectively, but my support for their appointment is solely with a view to making boards work better. I have no interest whatsoever in promoting the appointment of outside directors for political or decorative purposes.

His thoughts were echoed by Sir John Harvey-Jones when he was chairman of ICI:

> Despite the fact that I have very distinguished non-executive directors on my board, I have genuinely and honestly not appointed a single one because of his distinction. I have appointed them because they have personal or business qualities and knowledge that I need.

During his period as chairman, Sir John, in a typical act of pragmatism, invited Shoici Saba, president and chief executive of the Toshiba Corp of Japan to become a non-executive director on ICI's board. Saba was the first senior Japanese industrialist to sit on the board of the major UK company.

ICI recognised that the Far East was becoming an increasingly important market for the company and that it needed top-level advice on how to exploit that potential. Noted Sir John at the time: 'All of us who have worked and sold there know that things look very different through Japanese eyes. So we thought it would be very helpful if we had somebody over there who could actually give us a Japanese perspective.'

Dr Anna Mann, who runs a leading London-based headhunting firm that recruits senior executives in the £40,000 plus salary bracket, has observed a marked change in the requirements major companies are stipulating for non-executive directors:

> The important factor now is not who the person is, but what can he contribute. Companies are seeking younger men who are currently holding positions as chief executive of perhaps substantial organisations and where they have specific experience in areas that are relevant to the company concerned. They are seeking people with track records, people who can demonstrate performance achievement, people with energy, pace and drive. It doesn't matter where these people come from or what their social or educational backgrounds are, so long as they demonstrate that they can do something for the business.

Although an increasing number of companies are being more selective about the non-executive directors they appoint, some people feel the process still needs to be more formalised. Lord Ezra, former chairman of the Coal Board who is now a non-executive director on the boards of several leading UK and European companies, is convinced the system is still too haphazard and that the role of the non-executive director is ill-defined.

> I believe the non-executive director has a very positive role to play in Britain, but we need to rethink that role. The trouble in this country is that we have not given sufficient regard to what the non-executive director is meant to do. I have experienced enormous variations: people who are just brought on by the chairman because they happen to be pals; people who are brought on because it is felt they can make a positive contribution; people who are deluged with paper; people who are starved of paper; people who are brought into discussions; people who are not brought into discussions. The variations are endless.

Lord Ezra would like to see a set of guidelines drawn up which would clearly outline exactly what is expected of non-executive directors and the role they should play. The guidelines should also, in his view, advise on the right mix between executive and non-executive directors. When he was chairman of the Coal Board Lord Ezra presided over a twelve-man board that was equally split between executive and non-executive directors. He found that an ideal mix. He is convinced that a lot more structure could be adopted without going to the extreme of mandatory controls.

> We seem to be bemused in this country with saying everybody should do whatever they like and the result is we are getting poorer results from the benefits we could get from non-executive directors. There ought to be properly enunciated rules laid down by the CBI or the IOD or the Bank of England – somebody like that. I'm not talking about statutory controls or anything like that, which are to be avoided if at all possible.

Although entrepreneurs and professional managers differ in their approach, many of the qualities needed to manage successfully are common to both. All of the industrial leaders interviewed for this book regarded getting along with colleagues and the motivation of the work-force as a high priority. Sir Francis Tombs believes that man-management is one of the most vital skills needed by a senior executive, while Sir Graham Wilkins of Thorn EMI credits his success at the top largely to a facility for getting on with people. Explains Tombs:

> I make a practice of talking to people who work for me, looking at them and seeing how they react – whether they're unduly pale, whether they're tired or twitchy. I make a practice of being interested in their home life. All those things come into it a lot.

Wilkins puts great store by being able to get people 'not only to work for me, but to enjoy working for me. It's either something you've got or you haven't.' Sir Hector Laing maintains it is necessary 'to have a work-force that believes in you. Therefore, you've got to give it leadership and you've got to be seen. I think a business can hardly fail if it's got that sort of spirit. If the work-force is working against you, it can hardly win.' A similar view is held by Sir Alan Dalton, former chairman of English China Clays.

> People respond better if they understand what the problems are and have an opportunity to contribute. If I've had any effect at all in a key position in my professional life it has been to try to emphasise the fact that if you're employing five thousand people it is not just their arms and legs, it's their heads and hearts as well and that it is vital to get the whole man or woman involved in the solution rather than becoming part of the problem.

Many successful top executives go to great lengths to motivate their staff. One of them is Tony Berry, chairman of Blue Arrow, the world's biggest recruitment agency: 'Everyone at Blue Arrow is on incentives, from the newest girl to each company's managing director. All the incentives are performance-related, against budget and market conditions.' He believes that whether or not people are financially aware, they like to know how their company is performing. 'So the most important thing is to put in financial controls and get reports. If a girl is responsible for permanent placements in a City branch of Brook Street, she knows how that branch has done each week.'

Alan Sugar, the self-made millionaire entrepreneur who heads electronics group Amstrad, stresses the importance of good internal communications by keeping the work-force lean. His five key managers all sit together in an open-plan office where they can call across to each other directly. Sugar himself occupies an armchair in the middle of the floor – the only outward sign of his chairman and chief-executive status. 'We don't have six or seven executives per department; we have one working at full steam.' His emphasis on internal communication is in strict contrast to his attitude to external relations. City analysts, for example, compare him to a recluse Trappist monk in the way he rejects any rapport with the outside world. Sugar believes he has good reason for an aloof posture. 'Why should I waste my time talking to people who can write a report knocking thirty per cent off Amstrad's capitalisation?'

Someone who puts an equally high premium on the work-force is Sir Monty Finniston, the former British Steel chief:

> People are the only appreciating asset you have in a business. All the other assets disappear; you write them off. You depreciate them every year. In five years a machine is counted as nothing in the balance sheet, but your people count and age makes them more experienced, gives them better judgement – if they're capable of learning, which most people are.

Good man-management is something that Sir Charles Villiers, another former British Steel chairman, believes British industry as a whole has neglected to its cost. In his book *Start Again Britain* he questions whether British industrialists have got their priorities right and makes out a powerful case for emulating the Japanese approach.

> In Britain the top priority in the manager's mind is the cult of management - how do I manage? What are the problems of management itself? The preservation of management too is right at the very top. Next comes the shareholders because it is argued that in theory the business belongs to the shareholders and they are the only people who can get rid of us. After that comes the customers. They're a frightful nuisance, but you've got to have them. Last of all comes the work-force. They are regarded as machine-minders; they're a commodity you can hire and fire.
>
> That's what we've all been brought up to. It comes from the old Jewish tradition that was carried into Christianity and very strongly emphasised by the Calvanist and Protestant ethic. It really is the standard – what really happens, quite apart from what people say. It worked quite well until the Far East, particularly the Japanese, came into the big industrial picture.

Villiers points out that the Japanese business ethic has quite different roots based on Confucian, Taoist and Shintoist traditions. These put heavy emphasis on loyalty, benevolence and harmony. The former steel chief is frequently in touch with industrial leaders in Japan and he identifies a completely different set of priorities in the East.

> The top priority is really the work-force – its performance, its well being, its attitude, its co-operation, its loyalty, its satisfaction, all the things connected with that. Next to that comes the customer and the customer's exact requirements.
>
> The third priority in the East is the management. They take a lot of trouble over management training and ensuring it's the right sort of management. They don't like managers being too prominent. They have a great saying that the nail that sticks up will be hammered down. So you get a very grey, but definitely very strong, consensus management style. The fourth priority, is the shareholder, who is regarded as somebody who is rather necessary – and if there is anything left over he can have it. They plough nearly everything back into the business before the shareholder gets anything, so that the investment programme can benefit. The shareholder accepts that and is prepared to take one per cent yield or a half per cent yield. That's why the Tokyo share market hasn't collapsed. They're in it for the long term. They never expect to make money instantly.

The companies that show the most compassion towards their employees tend to be the family firms which have a corporate responsibility tradition going back several generations, although even many of them have had to bow to the necessity of mass lay-offs dictated by today's harsh economic climate. But in the modern world it is often difficult to draw the line between being a good corporate citizen and being paternalistic. Sir Alan Dalton, who used to run English China Clays, a company that provides jobs for more than five thousand employees in and around St Austell in Cornwall, does not believe that paternalism is anything to be ashamed of.

> If paternalism means we are concerned about people and families, the communities in which we are living and working, yes we are paternalistic. If paternal means anything, it

> means you take a sensible and responsible interest in the people you have bred and are rearing.

But paternalism, like everything else, has to adapt to the times. It was once customary at Cadbury's for all new recruits to spend a day a week on a company training programme, which was compulsory. In the 1960s however, the programme had to be made optional because it was proving a hindrance to recruitment. Sir Adrian similarly believes that a company's responsibility to the community at large needs to recognise changing circumstances:

> In one sense, businesses are licensed by the community to operate and you have to work within the terms of the licence which tend to change. You have to keep in tune with the changes. After all, it wasn't that long ago that it was quite acceptable to belch smoke over the countryside. The responsibility can be defined differently at different periods of time.

There is no doubt in Sir Francis Tombs's mind about what corporate responsibility entails:

> The principal responsibility is to employ people in a fair way. In that I include fair rates of pay, conditions of work, training, provision of sports and social facilities and helping people when they become redundant. I also believe in companies supporting charities, but they should be related to the business you are in.

In Sir Hector Laing's view, every chief executive should set down, as he has done at United Biscuits, exactly what his company's responsibility to the community should be. 'He should make it known within the company that this is one of his priorities, that the whole board supports it and that a percentage of the profits should be devoted to it.'

Some top managers are convinced that a company's corporate responsibility stance is so important that it is something that should be defined and articulated in a mission statement. Notes Sir Adrian: 'It's very difficult to do, because if you aren't careful you just write down a series of platitudes, but I think it is very necessary even if it does look platitudinous.'

In a fast-moving world, deciding long-term strategy has become increasingly difficult. Sir Monty Finniston has abandoned the idea that it is possible to predict the future with any degree of accuracy.

> I used to believe it was possible to make forecasts – market forecasts in particular – which were likely to be accurate. I no longer believe solely in figures. I believe in sensitivity analyses and I believe in ranges. But I've come to the conclusion that these are sometimes a bit astrological, particularly if you're in a competitive situation. You've got to know what your rivals are doing.

Nor does Sir Francis Tombs believe that computers have done much to help top managers make important decisions about long-term strategy.

> One of the great problems with engineering and management is the advent of the computer which churns out numerical data that is only as good as the input. People tend to compile a whole spectrum of scenarios and a whole spectrum of variances until I say they present you with a choice ranging from zero to infinity.

Every industrial leader has his own technique for tackling major business decisions. Sir Francis Tombs tends to solve a difficult issue by 'kicking it around'. He once got about twenty of his key people together in a room and discussed a thorny problem for two days. 'Gradually the picture became clearer and clearer . . . The other thing I find very important is not to rush vital decisions, because I find the subconscious works wonders.' Sir Hector Laing also believes in 'chewing over' major decisions and likes to talk them through with colleagues.

> I will sometimes arrange to discuss things on three successive Mondays, for example, or three successive months perhaps, because you never have to take a quick decision in a business, and out of the talking with people who respond

> to your way of working, the right answer very often comes – the decisions mostly take themselves.

Other senior managers prefer to work things out methodically on paper. Sir Adrian Cadbury, for example, favours this systematic approach and is not a great believer in intuition or acting on impulse.

> I would find it very hard to follow gut feel if I could not put forward arguments on two sides of a sheet of paper as to why it was the right decision . . . I like, before coming to a decision, to get the arguments down on paper and it seems to me if you can't then convince yourself or anybody else that what you propose is logically right, it doesn't much matter what your gut's doing.

Eddy Shah, the newspaper entrepreneur, argues that the importance of making the right decisions can in any case be over-emphasised. In an interview with *Your Business* magazine he insisted that it is commitment that counts. 'I bet you that fifty per cent of the decisions which have been looked on as great decisions over the years were the wrong ones at the time.' Shah maintained it isn't getting the decisions right that makes top executives successful. It is the hard work they put into implementing them that counts. 'Look at the people who have achieved success. People like Murdoch. Suddenly the name is there, but they haven't been an overnight success. It took Murdoch fourteen years to build News International up to what it is now.'

Sir John Harvey-Jones is equally insistent that top executives should not be too dogmatic in their outlook, as he explained in an interview with a business magazine when he was still the head of ICI.

> I'm not a very black and white manager. I'm black and white in the objective, but I'm very flexible in how we achieve the objective. With a large organisation, the correct way is to have absolute clarity of the overall aim, and then leave it to the chaps to get on with it.

Although most top executives agree that the ability to analyse problems rationally, a technique often derived from a university education or scientific training, Sir Francis Tombs believes it would be wrong to eliminate an element of entrepreneurial flair from the equation.

> You have to be prepared as a professional manager occasionally to take chances . . . I think a lot of professional managers look down on the term 'entrepreneur', because they regard it as synonymous with chance. I don't think you can just be a professional manager. You must have flair; you must be prepared to exploit opportunities.

What all successful top executives seem to agree on, however, is that once having reached an important decision it should be implemented decisively and that the top man should never shy away from the consequences of the decision, however painful they might be. According to Sir Austin Pearce,

> there's got to be determination, consistency, the ability to listen to other people and then make your mind up and stick to it. You can do it in a variety of ways. Some people would do it in a very extrovert way. That's not my way of doing it. I prefer to work quietly behind the scenes.

Sir Robert Haslam, chairman of British Coal, has always found implementing hard decisions involving employees the most difficult part of management.

> But you should never take the easy option . . . If you rationalise it by saying I don't want a row because I've got so much on my plate, it usually bounces back at you, often in an amplified form. If you cut corners just for a quiet life, you'll have trouble. It just builds up.

Practically every leading businessman maintains that there is no substitute for experience of the shop floor when starting out on a career in industry. Even those born into family firms swear by the importance of an initial stint at the bottom of the ladder, getting to know all the rudiments of the business. Sir Hector Laing recalls going into the bakery with his father when only five to get his first whiff of what a major food manufacturer is all about.

> Part of the advice one would want to give to any young person today is to thoroughly know your business by working on the factory floor. I came to understand fully about making biscuits and if you make things right you have a chance of selling them – as the Japanese have amply demonstrated. If you fail to make them right, then all the marketing and computers in the world won't help you.

Similarly, Sir Adrian Cadbury benefitted immensely from a basic training that had him rotating between all the different business sectors when he first joined the family firm. 'I spent the first eighteen months working in all the factory departments, so I started with a good knowledge of precisely how the product was made and did all the jobs that then existed in the production of confectionery.' When Sir Austin Pearce was put in charge of the Fawley refinery for Esso at the ripe old age of twenty-nine, he found himself on shift with men who were a lot older and more experienced than himself. It taught him, among other things, 'the realisation that the chap on the shop floor usually knows far more about what's going on than management does.'

A lot of up-and-coming young executives set their sights too high in the early stages of their career, in Sir Francis Tombs's experience. He is critical of the over-ambitious promotion graphs many of them draw up at a very premature stage. 'They ought to be approaching the issue from the other view entirely. They should be working like hell at their jobs, trying to demonstrate they know what they're doing and hoping to be recognised through that route and then looking for opportunities. You can't predestine a plan.' Suggests Sir Adrian Cadbury: 'You need to find out what you're good at; you need to find out what it is you can contribute which other people can't and that is something which only you can find out for yourself.'

Peter de Savary suggests that before an aspiring executive gains experience of the world and the business environment, it is necessary to,

> come to terms with yourself on certain fundamental principles which you have to believe in and live by in your

> career. Otherwise the experience you may gain from seeing the world and travelling and doing whatever you might do will be somewhat wasted.

The first prerequisite, in de Savary's view, is to be honest with yourself . . . Never be afraid to say: I screwed up.

Sticking to an agreement is a quality that Blue Arrow's Tony Berry puts great store by. 'Never go back on your word – if you say it's a deal, it's a deal, even if you've made a mistake. I have a reputation for being totally honest and fairly straightforward. Also, I'm not particularly bright, so people feel comfortable when they talk to me.'

Harry Goodman, who left school without any O or A levels but went on to create the fast-growing International Leisure Group, maintains that self-confidence is vital when setting out to build a business empire. He admitted in an interview with *Your Business* magazine that it was not easy, with his lack of education, to approach leading banks for financial support in the early days.

> You're not human unless you've got a lot of self-doubt. But you mustn't show it. When new boys are coming up, the City takes advantage of that. What you've got to do is remember you're dealing with another human being who may or may not be brighter than you, and if you're running your own business and are halfway successful, it's odds-on you're brighter than him.

Unlike professional top managers, who have usually had a university education, entrepreneurs seem to thrive on poor school results. Peter de Savary left school at sixteen with only one O level – in scripture. It was a great motivator. 'I was a dismal failure at school. That didn't please me . . . and I set out to prove that I could do something successfully.' Neither does youthful entrepreneur Richard Branson have any regrets about missing out on a university education.

> I learned my entrepreneurship by having to survive. By not going to university I missed out on the chance to read

> more books, listen to records and have a nice social life, but I am very happy with the way my life has gone. If I had gone to university I suspect my career would have taken a different course. I always wanted to be a journalist.

In an article in the *Sunday Times* Professor Alan Budd of the London Business School even suggests that a university education could be a handicap to potential entrepreneurs. 'I can well imagine that the flair and originality of some highly successful entrepreneurs might have been harmed by going to university. They have their own internal genius which has to be allowed to flower in its own way.'

Few senior executives accept that it is any harder today to be a top industrialist than it used to be, despite the faster pace of change and the complexities of global markets. Sir Francis Tombs considers the advantages and disadvantages of operating at the top today tend to balance out. 'There are elements of complexity and there are elements of simplification. Britain used not to be a particularly powerful exporting nation, except to the tied markets of the Commonwealth. Now we are in competition with the rest of the world.'

Notes Sir Austin Pearce: 'You've got to deal with different problems, there's no question about that. They're on a worldwide scale rather than a national scale, but you have to recognise that there are only so many hours in the day in which you can be efficient.'

What sort of industrial climate awaits tomorrow's senior executive? If all the current trends continue, it could be foreseen as a rather forbidding future in which moral decline, short-term expediency, automation and the post-industrial society dominate. But today's top industrialists are inclined to take a more optimistic view. Sir Adrian Cadbury is very suspicious of the predicted shift towards service industries away from manufacturing. 'I'm sceptical about what post-industrial means. It sounds suspiciously like getting everything without working for it. I think the fundamentals will stay the same.'

Sir Monty Finniston is equally sanguine. 'You can't afford the service industries unless you've got a good manufacturing base . . . But the only appreciating resource that we've got is the talents and skills of the people to design, to manufacture, to produce and provide a service.' Sir Adrian Cadbury believes that the key to success in the future will revolve around a more flexible working life in which employment, education and training are all intermingled. He sees this as the only way to distribute the enormous amount of work that needs to be done. 'It's absurd really to say that because of automation there is less and less work when you see how much there is that needs doing in the community. I think we will balance work and leisure in a totally different way.'

Whatever the future economic climate turns out to be, the qualities needed to take ambitious executives to the top are unlikely to change very dramatically. Lord King, the chairman of British Airways, summed them up as 'vision, ambition and hard work' in an address to a group of high fliers who had taken part in a business competition sponsored by the charity Young Enterprise. He left them with some interesting thoughts to ponder on. 'Young men see visions; old men dream dreams . . . It is the vision which generates the determination and the dream which sustains the years of hard work.'

Index

INDEX